A WATERSIDE YEAR

By Fennel Hudson:

A MEANINGFUL LIFE
A WATERSIDE YEAR
A WRITER'S YEAR
WILD CARP
FLY FISHING
TRADITIONAL ANGLING
THE QUIET FIELDS
FINE THINGS
A GARDENER'S YEAR
THE LIGHTER SIDE
FRIENDSHIP
NATURE ESCAPE
BOOK OF SECRETS
THE PURSUIT OF LIFE

Fennel's Journal

No. 2

A WATERSIDE YEAR

By

Fennel Hudson

2025

FENNEL'S PRIORY LIMITED

Published by Fennel's Priory Limited

www.fennelspriory.com

First shared as handwritten letters in 2007
Limited edition magazine published in 2012
eBook published in 2013
This first edition hardback published in 2025

Copyright © Fennel Hudson 2007, 2025

A CIP catalogue record for this book
is available from the British Library.

ISBN 978-1-909947-06-1

Available to purchase in other formats at
www.fennelspriory.com

Designed and typeset in 12pt Adobe Garamond Premier Pro.

CONTENTS

STOP – UNPLUG – ESCAPE – ENJOY

This book, and the series to which it belongs, is about freedom. It's also about the adventures to be had when pursuing one's dreams, developing and communicating one's self, and striving for a slow-paced rural life.

Fennel's Journal is your opportunity to take time out from the stresses of modern living, to stop the wheels for a while, unplug from the daily grind, escape to a quiet and peaceful place, and enjoy the simple life. Because of this, it should ideally be read in a distraction-free and relaxing environment: your 'safe place' where you can savour quality time and, if possible, delight in the beauty of the countryside.

That's why this book is pocket-sized, has a special waxy cover, and is printed using waterproof ink. It's designed to be taken with you on your travels. Don't store it in pristine condition upon a bookshelf; allow it to reflect the adventures you've had. Use a leaf as a bookmark and annotate the pages with ideas of how you will honour your right to 'never do anything that offends your soul'.

The more mud-splattered, grass-stained, and ink-scribbled this book becomes, the more you've demonstrated your ability to pursue a contented country life. So go on: live your life, be authentic, and always remember to 'Stop – Unplug – Escape – Enjoy'.

"My chief delight was in nature, and when I opened a book it was to find something about nature in it, especially some expression of the feeling produced in us by nature, which was, to me, the most important thing in life."

W. H. Hudson

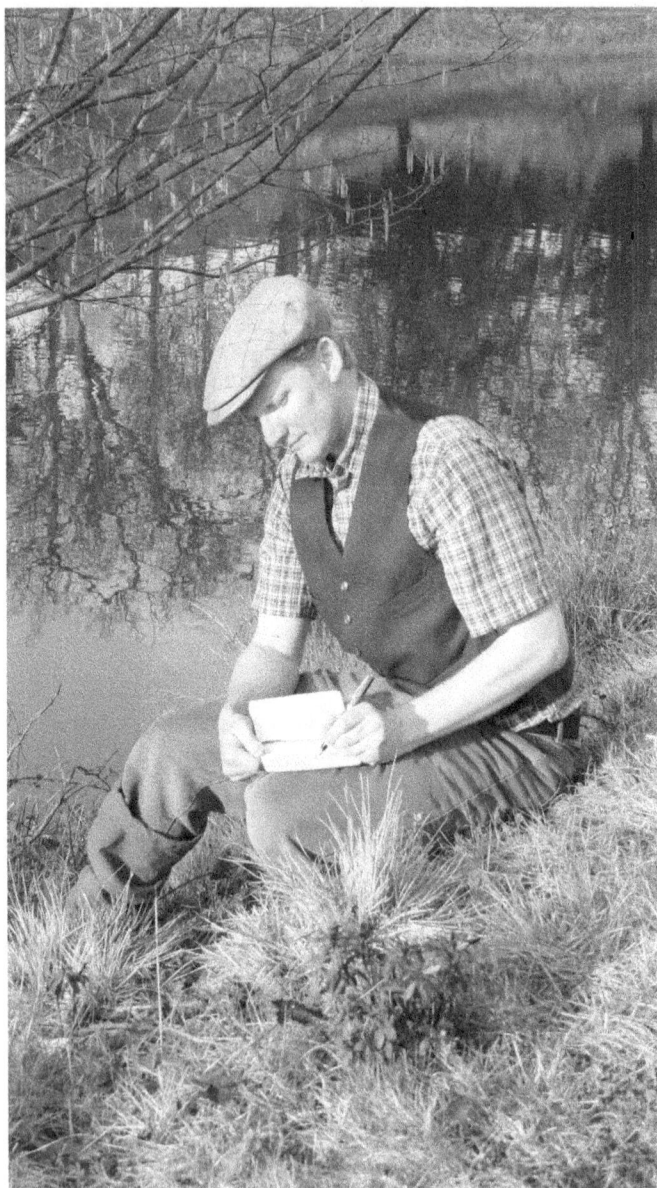

INTRODUCTION

Welcome to the water's edge, a place where reeds rustle in the breeze and a tweed-wearing countryman sits and writes these words. This edition of Fennel's Journal chronicles a year when I sought 'time out' to rediscover my roots. I'd spent the previous year 'finding myself', using the process to document the values and character of something that became known as Fennel's Priory. I was (and still am) committed to the ideals of the Priory, which are captured in the motto 'Stop – Unplug – Escape – Enjoy'. But in 2007 I took the words rather too literally and decided to turn my back on society, to exist alone in a wood beside a lake. A Thoreauvian lifestyle, you might think. And you'd be partly right. But I wasn't running away, and I wasn't entirely isolated. I still had work obligations and, in September, got married to Mrs H-to-Be. I just needed time on my own to reflect on things past, present, and future.

I spent the spring, summer and autumn months living in a lakeside tent. Doing so was enabled by a new job that allowed me to 'work from home'. Instead of cooping myself up indoors, I opted for the relative discomfort of musky canvas and a damp sleeping bag. And within them I would write article after article

for my new employer, delivering the files during my infrequent visits to the office. My remaining time (most of it) was spent studying the wildlife of the pool. I lived free from the hands of a watch, spending my days and nights in idle fashion. Generally speaking, I lived the life of a tramp. I foraged and hunted food, washed in the outflow stream, fished in the lake, explored the woods and fields during the day and wrote by candlelight at night. It was the most basic yet rewarding existence.

The lake was several miles from the nearest road, so I was undisturbed by visitors other than anglers, farm workers and Mrs H-to-Be (who visited at weekends). I was able to live harmoniously alongside the animals, fishes, birds, and plants of the lake and woods.

I didn't so much study them, as co-exist with them. I found freedom in their company and concluded that rural places, and the life they contain, are worth living for. And in doing so, our lives are shaped for the better. Yet what I learned about my surroundings was diminished by what I learned about myself.

Spending so much time alone, when I already had the beginnings of an idyllic home life, was a questionable move. For consider: where was my heart during all of this? Was I being overly selfish and obsessive? And what was I trying to prove? Was my mission really to become a complete layabout? Or was I just a jammy so-and-so with time on his hands and a very understanding fiancée? To find out, you'll have to read the Journal, and see where it leads.

Here are the stories from a very special year.

I

A LAKE WITH A PURPOSE

Water, it is said, has the power to heal. It can quench a thirst, cleanse a wound and soothe a burn. But its healing properties extend beyond these obvious medical benefits. Water, you see, is *magical*.

If you've ever spent time gazing into a stream, river, pond or ocean, you'll know that water can calm your thoughts and relax your body. It helps you to unwind. It can lull you into a peaceful state, or it can perk you up. It's the wonderment of water that makes it so appealing: thoughts of what's beneath the surface, or out there beyond a watery horizon. Maybe these thoughts are primeval, the dreams of our ancestors echoing in our subconscious? The urge we feel to 'set sail', to explore beyond the bend of a river, or across an estuary, or out to sea; it could be the distant hopes of our forefathers sounding in our minds. Because they knew, and we know, that water is intrinsically linked to the mystery and excitement of discovering new worlds. Of dreams. And hopes. And thoughts of what 'could be'. But as I said earlier, water is magical. You don't need a boat to explore its mystery. All you need is the ability to dream.

Imagine yourself paddling a boat across a calm sea. Water swirls from the movement of the oars, and you feel compelled to know what lives beneath its surface. You stand up and dive into the water, to swim among the hoped-for fishes. You see them, but wonder what lurks deeper still. You open your mouth and gulp down the salty water, drinking the ocean dry so you may see the lobsters and crabs scuttling across its muddy floor. In the dream world, anything is possible. It only requires a fertile imagination, and a desire to explore the half-light between the known and the unknown. (As with writing by candlelight, one's greatest ideas come from 'the flickering' between darkness and light.)

Dreams free us from normality. Daydreams, especially, take us somewhere between the real world and the dream world. I was once in great need of such a place. I'd survived an ordeal and needed somewhere quiet in which to recover. The Priory became this dream place, and as the daydreams grew longer, the distinction between what was real and what was imaginary grew less. Soon I existed in a blissful world of my own creation; somewhere I could choose my emotional state based upon the strength of the Priory lens and my desire to escape or conform.

You might think that craving escapism is dangerous, that it is too removed from normality. I assure you that it is not, as being distanced from normality is the entire point of what I seek to achieve. (At least the normality of normal folk leading normal lives and being boringly normal.) I want to view the world in a way that means something 'more'. A different and more interesting view. Whether this is achieved through escapism or reality is not my call to make. Because what I've learned is that

A LAKE WITH A PURPOSE

reality is just a matter of perception.

The degree to which we notice the obvious or the subtle, and the angle of light that we see falling upon it, depends upon how closely we look and the time we spend studying. For example, do you know, to the nearest hundred, how many species of wild flowers live on a mile of motorway embankment? I'd guess there

are more than grow alongside a country lane. But we rarely have time to make time for such things, not that it would be especially safe to do so on a motorway.

Many people fear the unknown. They busy themselves at motorway speed so to excuse their lack of understanding of the world around them. "I don't have time for all that nonsense; it's just not important to me," they say. While they might know about politics, commerce and current affairs, they are feeding their knowledge on spoon-fed drivel downloaded from a news channel. It is not based on real and meaningful first-hand experience. Something we call *living*.

Knowledge gained via third parties is already filtered by their sense of what is real and what is important. Touching, smelling, hearing, tasting and *feeling* something creates greater understanding. It's this understanding that fascinates me. Why people interpret the same experience in different ways. Take these journals for example. They are first written in burgundy-brown ink using an antique fountain pen. I write into an old book that smells of dust and whose pages are floppy with damp. Sometimes the ink splodges onto the paper, other times it will barely leave the nib of my pen. Rarely will I write indoors, even if it means getting wet during rain, or my hands numb in winter. I could write the journals quicker and more comfortably using the computer in my study. But I don't. It's important to me that they are authentic, that they properly capture the moment, and that I understand – first hand – the events and emotions about which I'm writing. I'm sure that someone else would write, or type, in another way;

that they'd describe the events differently, or identify things that I've either not seen or have chosen to omit. This illustrates how choice and perception are closely linked. They are unique, personal and emotional. I *perceive* the Priory and these journals. They are my view of a life that is very real.

Life, as I see it, wraps around us, even when we think we are firmly embracing it. Reality is in the ether, a blend of present-day experiences infused with one's memories and dreams. A life that is real to one is surreal to another.

Have you ever shuffled a deck of cards by bending them at the corners and merging them together? Think of the satisfying 'brrrrp' they make and the flicker of images beneath your thumbs. Modern life is a bit like this – a blur and a 'brrrrp'. Sooner or later we are compelled to stop shuffling, to extract a card and hold it, calmly, for a while. Doing so gives us a break from life's fast-paced obligations. It provides us with a sense of pride; that we are in control, especially if it is the King of Hearts.

I stopped the shuffle recently, when I was confronted by a blur of flickering and conflicting 'priorities'. Each was apparently urgent and important. "Drop everything," I was told by a so-called superior, "and focus on this task, right now!" I did drop everything. I quit my job, returned home and decided with Mrs H-to-Be that the time was right for a change. A relocation and new career, to be specific. But these were just the first and obvious conclusions. The card I extracted from the chaos did not carry the image of a house particular or

a job advert, but rather an image of a lake. A lake of my childhood, where once I was free to be me, when I enjoyed a slow-paced life and was completely happy. The healing power of water had returned.

I knew what I had to do. I would seek out a lake, spend time by water, and wash away the anxieties and frustrations of working in a corporate world where I didn't belong. I'd return to my roots, where I could rediscover all that I once loved. This would be a valuable 'time out' of the rat race, where the dream of what is normal, right and beautiful would be properly savoured. First though, I had to find the lake: one so remote that it was ageless; so overgrown that it was forgotten, and so quiet that it was deafeningly serene. It would need to be a very special lake. A lake with a purpose.

II

PLUMBING THE DEPTHS

The problem with 1930s wiring is that you never know when it's going to pack up or burst into flames. One minute you can be happily listening to *Gardener's Question Time* on the radio, the next you can be calling the fire brigade and throwing your favourite books out of the window. I mention this because my home has such wiring.

I'm currently in the attic of my cottage, putting away the Christmas decorations for another year. There's a light above my head that flickers, dims, flashes and crackles as if it is about to zap me with some pre-war laser beam. It is my nemesis, challenging me to a standoff whenever I poke my head into the loft and flick the switch.

Putting all the tinsel and baubles away is something I do with mixed emotion. It marks the end of an eventful time but signifies hope for future festivities. Each year sees me do it more quickly than the last, not least because of the growing risk of electrocution from the bulb of horrors, which greets me with its usual twitching eye. This year, however, is different. Mrs H-to-Be and I have decided that a house move is in order and because of this I have to endure the gamma rays for longer than usual.

I am under strict instruction to catalogue the contents of the attic, so that we may plan the logistics of the move.

Sounds like an easy task? It would be if I could give Mrs H-to-Be a full account of the attic's contents. But I can't. The attic, as you will soon discover, is home to many things, not all of which are ours.

Mrs H-to-Be is a stickler for tidiness. Although she has a deep appreciation of heritage and sentiment, she draws the line much quicker than I do when it comes to what is valuable and what is junk. What she doesn't know is that up here, out of sight and duster, are twenty-two boxes left by the previous owner. In them are all manner of things that I find fascinating, but which she would long-since have banished to the rubbish dump. For example, one box is full of musky and yellowing newspapers from the 1950s. They look and smell like a vagrant's bedding, but their headlines are wonderful: "We've Never Had it so Good", "Everest Conquered", "Killer Fog Descends on London", "Bannister Beats the Four-Minute Mile". Another box contains electrical items: a toaster with a two-pin plug; a Bakelite telephone (with proper dial) whose bell still rings when I shake it; and a mysterious item that looks like a cross between a Geiger counter and a walkie-talkie.

At the front of all the 'inherited' boxes is a much newer box, held together with plastic tape. It has the word 'sentiments' written upon it. This is my box, the one that has accompanied me on each of my house moves to date. It contains all manner of knickknacks, from ornaments inherited from my grandparents, to things I've held onto because they remind me of distinct periods of my life. There are things in there like a gas mantel, taken from the caravan where I spent my childhood holidays (and kept to remind me that electricity is a relatively modern luxury); my collection of pre-decimalisation coins, begged from relatives during the late 70s; and a rag-eared copy of the school newspaper that I once edited. I could go on, but I'm beginning to realise that I'm either overly sentimental, or am a hoarder who struggles to part with things. In all honesty, I'm probably both.

Strangely, I've just noticed that excluding the Christmas decorations, there are twenty-four boxes in this attic. An extra box has just been illuminated by a rather angry fizzle from the demon above. The box looks familiar, but its contents haven't been viewed in over twenty years. I shall go and investigate.

I felt my hair lift as I passed the light bulb on my way to the box. The rafters groaned and juddered as I traversed my way across the floor, passing three bird nests and an unusually stiff dead mouse that, although hunched over, was most definitely grinning. (I concluded that its final seconds of life were very happy.) Who would have thought that so many creatures were living such contented lives above our heads? I will have to start charging them rent.

So, to the box. It is marked KFS. My old fishing club. The club I ran as secretary from 1990 to 1993. Hmm. Now this is the sort of treasure I like.

Wait one minute…

"What's that dear? Taking too long? Reading

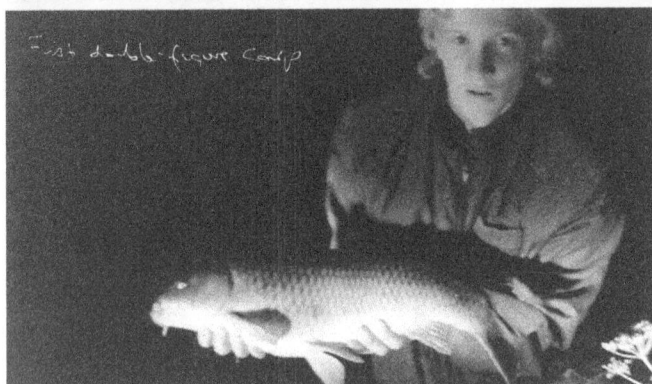

magazines? No, no. Just boxes. I need to know what's in the boxes..."

Apologies for that. Where was I? Oh yes. The KFS box. KFS (which stands for Kinver Fishing Syndicate) was the club that held the fishing rights to my favourite childhood lake – a two-acre pond in Shropshire. It was there that I learned to fish and where most of my earliest memories are centred. It held many finned species, but the dominant fish were carp. Not the bulging, greying and scaleless creatures prevalent in many lakes today, but rather the sleek, golden-scaled and truly beautiful wild carp that had inhabited the lake for centuries.

I have just opened the KFS box. This time capsule contains many years of memories: a book of catch returns, a photo album and a rolled up map.

I am looking at the photo album as I write these words. My, how young I look. The first photos are dated 1982. I am eight years old, proudly holding a trout that, I'm sure, was caught by my father. Ah. I'm a bit older in the next one. It's inscribed on the back: "First carp, 1989, five pounds, sweetcorn, float, by weedbed". Another reads, "First double-figure carp", although by the look of it the fish, it must have been wearing lead fins when I weighed it. There are other photos in there too, of the lake and its wildlife. These images are from a time when I would get the bus home from school, quickly collect my fishing tackle and then cycle to the lake so that I could be there for when the carp started basking near the surface in the late afternoon light.

The returns book shows that most fishing was done between mid-July and early September. Many of the club's members were teachers, so it's not surprising that most fished in the school holidays. Bream, roach, perch and gudgeon are mentioned, though carp feature most. Yet I don't recollect the pool ever being thought of as a carp fishery. Such terms were reserved for bigger waters, with bigger fish and anglers with bigger egos. The Cottage Pool, as the water was affectionately known, was just a pond where anglers came to fish. There was never discussion about which species they were fishing for. It was the place, and the act of angling, that appealed.

Finally, to the rolled up map. To view this properly, I must climb down from the attic and study it in daylight. I will give one last confrontational squint at the epileptic strobe above, then dust myself off, cough like a chain-smoking turtle and dodge my way back to the glow of light in the corner of the floor.

I am downstairs now, in the kitchen with Mrs H-to-Be, who has remarked that I either have a bad case of dandruff or have decided to head-butt a bag of flour. I've reassured her that my appearance is merely the aftermath of a mouse's orgy with three starlings. The shaking of her head indicates that she wished she hadn't asked.

Mrs H-to-Be and I have rolled out the map on the kitchen table, and have held down its corners with teacups. It's been eleven years since I last saw this map. Seeing it makes my hairs bristle and my eyes water. It is a plan of The Cottage Pool, drawn by me when I was studying garden design at university. On it are marked the lake's main features – trees, weed beds, paths and fishing locations – but its main purpose was to record

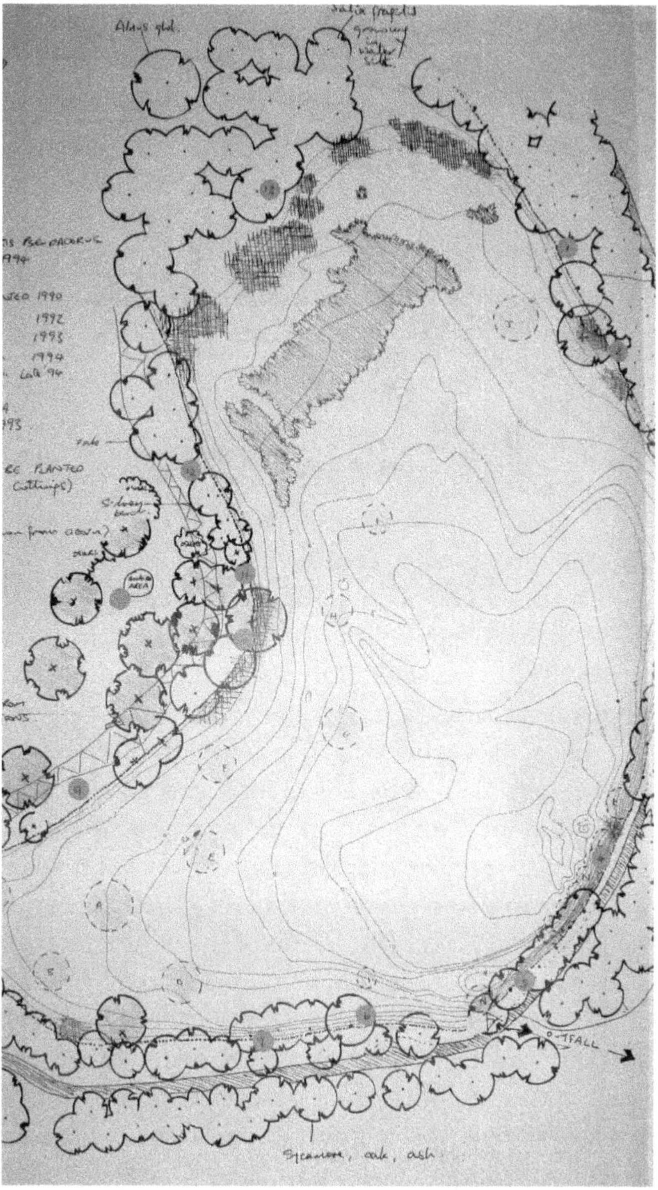
Alnus glut.
Salix fragilis growing in water
1990
1992
1993
1994
OUTFALL
Sycamore, oak, ash

the contours of the lakebed. Looking at the map I can see that the deepest point of the lake is, predictably, near to the dam. A depth of thirteen feet is recorded. Most of the lake, however, is relatively shallow, with depths averaging six feet.

I remember measuring the contours of the pool one winter's day when home for Christmas. I went out in a punt, armed with a three lengths of garden cane lashed together with twine. The pole was marked with dabs of paint, colour coded every twelve inches. I would row eight feet (the length of the punt) and then plunge the cane down through the water to the bottom of the lake, so to measure the depth. I did this, going up and down the lake for about five hours. Eventually I had a complete grid of measurements, from which I was able to trace the contours of the lakebed. The map pleased my college tutor and fascinated me at the time.

Now, however, it makes me want to break that blasted bamboo pole over my knee, as what the plan really marks is the turning point when the lake went from being a magical, mysterious place to one that was 'scientifically undone'. *It's not always best to know what's going on beneath the surface.* A pool has to have its secrets, and should never become too familiar; else one's love for it will dwindle. In my enthusiasm, I'd reduced The Cottage Pool to a grid of meaningless numbers connected by wavy lines.

Mrs H-to-Be has detected my sombre state. Her hand has just reached for mine, and she indicated that the map should be returned to the loft, an act of raising it higher, out of sight, so that it may fall and sink into memory. "There's something else, isn't there?" she enquired. I nodded and explained that I'd hoped to show her the lake of my childhood, where once I was most happy. But it was not to be. The Cottage Pool was no longer, I feared, the pool it once was. Too many years had passed. I had changed; it most probably had changed. I wasn't ready to go back there.

"Well then," said my beloved, "we'll just have to find another Cottage Pool."

It sounded almost too easy…

III

THIS LAKE IN WINTER

I am standing upon the dam of a lake, looking out across an expanse of white, non-reflecting water. I know there's a pool there – a line of trees and reed stems indicates this – and yet a lone pheasant is walking across what would be the middle of the lake and in the distance the water appears to be flowing up into the trees. Last night's frost has frozen everything, including the surface of this lake, which is now sleeping beneath a blanket of silent white.

I've been here for twenty minutes, gazing at the winterscape, watching my breath rise beyond the peak of my cap and wondering what fish lurk beneath the ice. The pheasant (which doesn't look too happy with its location) is the first creature I've seen in this otherwise desolate place. It seems the crisp air has encouraged the wildlife to stay indoors, and that only mad Englishmen and foreign birds brave the icicles of midwinter.

I'd planned to get here earlier than this (it is mid-morning) but the hard frost and remnants of yesterday's snow meant that I couldn't drive my car along the track to the pool. Instead, I parked by the side of the road and walked ('crump-crumping' through the snow) across three fields, through two woods and along a stream.

The walk took over an hour, and made me feel like I could melt the frost just by looking at it. I loosened my collar and stood back to admire the view.

Here I am, standing in the snow, writing with a pencil because the ink in my pen is frozen, about to introduce you to the lake that will become my home for a year. First, let me bring you up to speed with developments.

A lot has happened in the past month. I've worked my notice, put our cottage up for sale, got a new job, binned my nylon suit and called in a favour with a local farmer. I was driven by a desire for change, to not end up in the same lifeless situation as before, where a request to give a sample of blood would become a dinner date with the corporate vampire. I needed to find a place where I could enjoy my spare time and live without the gnawing reality of compromise.

I heard about the lake last week, when a pint in my local turned into a five-hour session and a full-blown rant about the state of the nation. Paul the stockman overheard the commotion and told me of a lake on the farm where he worked. "Ittud be a drive," he said, "but it's reet priddy arn owt-a-way." A good sleep and two Aspirin later, and I was able to telephone the landowner about the lake. The outcome was that I would be allowed to camp in the woods next to the pool in return for working on his farm every Saturday. A syndicate controlled the fishing (the inevitable compromise) but the owner knew of a vacancy. A phone call to the syndicate leader, and a promptly signed cheque sent in the post, secured my membership. And I hadn't even visited the lake. Something deep within told me it was

the right thing to do. Hence my excitement walking here today, for this, my first visit.

I return to the scene before me: a lake of about ten acres, flanked on the left by beech, alder, thuja conifers and oak; and on the right by willow, alders and poplar. Branches stick up through the snow-covered ice, indicating fallen trees that line the margins of the lake. The far end of the lake adjoins woodland that stretches as far as the horizon. Closer in, I can see that each corner of the dam is fringed by reedmace and that the right bank has a thicket of bulrush running along it – each stem of which is frosted with ice.

This isn't a lake that immediately announces itself as an angling water. There's no car park, no visible 'pitches' from which to fish, no path around the lake and no 'private, keep out' signs. Actually, this doesn't look or feel like an obvious lake, either. This frost has softened it and the landscape, helping to blend the two together.

But I like the atmosphere of the pool – it has a shy and retiring character, not wanting to cause any bother, just happy to be left alone. I can relate to this.

I know from my conversation with the syndicate leader that the lake contains roach, perch, pike, eels, tench, bream and carp. Most of the anglers fish only for the carp. Sadly, the syndicate leader mentioned that the lake was recently stocked with fast growing mirror carp, "Because the members were plagued by thin little wild carp". I could have chewed my fist into a pulp at hearing this news. (Why is it that so many syndicates and clubs insist on picking on the weak? Blinded by their obsession with big fish, they are prepared to irreversibly ruin the genetic strain of the fish for which they are responsible. *Fools. Blasted fools.* But the damage is done. The syndicate can fish for their 'plastic' blubbery stocked fish, and I will find quiet corners where I will attempt to get close to the remaining original carp.)

Which brings me to my plan. It is now late February. There are another three weeks left of the coarse fishing season, after which the lake will be undisturbed by anglers for three months. It is during this time, once the weather warms up, that I will begin my life beside the pool. I will find an open glade in the wood at the far end of the lake in which to erect my tent. I will bring with me enough supplies to live without having to venture into the outside world. I will observe the landscape during its seasonal transitions. I'll draw what I see and write about what I observe. I will leave my watch at home. The warmth of the sun will govern my daytime activities; my nights will be inspired by the brilliance of stars. I will close the farm gate behind me, disappearing into a warm and humid wood to live a simple life. Then, once a month, I will walk two miles to the nearest road, where I will find a post box to send these journals.

This peaceful pond will be my place of refuge, a new manifestation of the Priory. I'll stay here until my house is sold, when I'll begin a new life in a new part of the country. But first, I need to waterproof my tent and sew-up the mouse holes in my sleeping bag. I'm going camping!

MARCH

IV

A LAKESIDE CAMP

Well, this is it. Our time by the lake begins. (I say 'our' time, because, as Lord Byron wrote, "Letter writing is the only device for combining solitude with good company".) Mrs H-to-Be, who brought me here, has helped me unload my camping and 'survival' gear and has now departed for some 'quality time' at home. I have carried everything up into the woods, set up camp, got a fire started and made a brew. I am now sitting on a carpet of beech and oak leaves, with notepad on my knee, pen in hand and a mug of tea on the ground beside me. The disturbance of my arrival has subsided. Calm has descended and I feel at one with my new surroundings.

It's amazing how quickly this wood and the lake have welcomed my presence. I've camped in similar places before, often detecting a coldness that targets one's spine and makes it difficult to properly relax. Not so today. Today the air is fresh and inviting. I want to hold my hands aloft and smile. For I am free. A good start, given that I've only been here for a few hours.

I set up camp, as planned, in a small clearing in the woods. A vast tree stump (the diameter of which must be five feet) marks the centre of the clearing. I intend to use it as a dining table for when I'm feeling civil, but for now it is the gravestone of a once-mighty beech that grew here. Next to the stump is my tent: a two-man ex-army canvas job that, I'm pleased to say, has a built-in groundsheet. My tent doesn't look like much but, as an estate agent might say, "It is air-conditioned and with exceptional location." Inside is stored a canvas rucksack, brass Primus stove, Billy cans, Kelly Kettle, Tilley lamp, bow saw, tinned food, chorizo sausages, two loaves of bread, six pounds of butter, two-dozen eggs, quart of milk, six writing pads, three reading books, a spare change of clothes, waterproofs, wellingtons, a sleeping bag, foam mattress and thirty-six rolls of toilet paper. Oh, and an air rifle for when I need to defend the camp from bloodthirsty wolves.

I mention the contents of my tent because I want to illustrate that I have brought only the basics and that, in adventurer terms, I am of the illusion that I am 'travelling light'. However, looking at the tent, I am now questioning whether I will be able to crawl inside it tonight. I also realise that I have forgotten to bring any fresh water (I've learned from experience that drinking lake water, even when boiled, has an effect on my digestive system similar to the movement of a hangman's trapdoor). I've also neglected to bring a toothbrush, towel, and – how could I have been so stupid – any alcohol whatsoever. My only vice is a caddy of leaf tea that I shall reserve for those special evenings when the light is 'just right', when the wood pigeons coo, and when the air is so still that the steam rising from my teacup drifts leisurely up through the branches

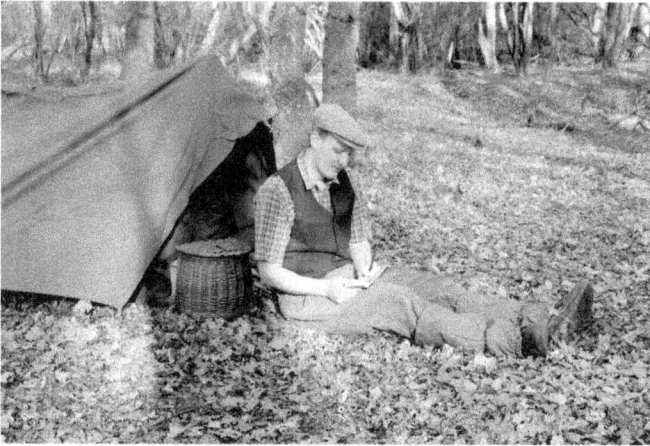

of the trees. Or I could just drink it all now and enjoy a caffeine rush that might last until morning.

My fishing tackle is stored outside the tent, although I don't have any intention of using it just yet (the coarse-fish season doesn't begin until the middle of June). However, it is possible to fish for trout at this time of year (their spawning has ended) and there's a trout stream nearby. So I'll probably seek my breakfast there. (First I'll gauge how often it's fished, and whether the keeper would mind me visiting every so often for 'essential sustenance', perhaps in exchange for a spare tin of beans or a damp loo roll.)

This camp isn't so much about logistics, as place. I've carefully chosen a spot that overlooks the lake. Here, the ground is much higher than down by the dam. I'd say about thirty feet higher, which enables me to look out across – and through – the treetops to the water below. The scene is so much different to our earlier visit. The snow has melted and the buds on the trees are swelling. The ground at the edge of the wood is carpeted with bluebells, although they look about three or four weeks away from flowering. The bird cherries are blossoming in the woods, marsh marigolds are out by the feeder stream, celandines are in bloom and arum lilies are in full leaf. The lake, in support of all the activity around it, looks like it could erupt at any moment. Its water is so very clear. Here and there are patches of bright green weed, visible in six feet of water. I can see roach dimpling the surface and carp basking in the sun. Coots and moorhens scuttle across the surface, defending their territories; a grebe is looking resplendent with its neck outstretched, attracting the ladies; and a bedraggled-looking heron stands in the sun, grateful to have made it through another winter.

Life in the wild, as I'm observing, is about survival as much as pleasure. I remember reading Thoreau's Walden where he speaks about keeping the internal fire going, and thinking it was merely the naïve thoughts of someone who lived in a less advanced medical age. But his were words of experience that, after my gruelling seven hours in the wilderness, I am beginning to see for their simple truth. I'm glad I packed that extra tin of chicken curry.

I might joke about my time here beside the lake, away from any likelihood of mobile phone signal or pizza delivery, but my being here is all about savouring the 'other life' that I once had, when I was younger and when days seemed to be filled with so much fun. I am, like that heron, grateful to be here. I'm grateful to be viewing such a picturesque scene and feeling so relaxed; I'm delighted to be out in the open air, hearing this fountain pen scratch across the page at an inspired speed. Being here is such a contrast to where I'd otherwise be. At this time (it is mid-afternoon) I'd normally be sitting at work, counting the keys on my computer keyboard, or making the twelfth phoney trip to the toilet (to kill time) or wondering why my email entitled "This is not My Life!" caused such uproar with Human Resources. But time is not something to be killed. Doing so suffocates a part of us, writing off part of our life that could, or rather should, be spent doing something meaningful. Like sitting beside a lake, writing and thinking about whatever springs to mind.

I am not at work, or at the supermarket, or waiting for a bus (metaphorically or otherwise). I am free. The final hours of the day will be spent gathering twigs for the Kelly Kettle and wood for the campfire. I might even go for a walk around the lake, to properly introduce myself, or I might leave that until tomorrow. I'm in no hurry. I might just sit here and watch the sun go down. And then I'll go to bed, to sleep the sleep of kings.

V

THE WILDLIFE OF A POND

I'm writing this with hands that are shaking and gripping my pen and pad so tightly that you'd think they were about to be yanked from my grasp. It is perhaps an hour or two after dark. I was happily sleeping, but was woken with a start by a raucous party going on outside my tent. There's no music, just the sound of fizzy beer being sipped from half-empty cans, followed by what I can only describe – in my stressed-out state – as faint, wet farts. I'm not entirely sure how close the intruders are to my tent, but I'm presented with a survival dilemma, somewhere between going outside in my underpants and confronting them with a super-cool "Hey guys, mind if I join the pardee?" and hiding in my sleeping bag and quivering until they go away. (After which I'd quietly pack up my tent and scarper.) The latter isn't really an option. My heart is beating so loudly that they'd be sure to hear me. I will have to brave it. First though, I must assess the situation in more detail. How many louts are we talking about? What size? What state of inebriation? How many pellets do I have for the air gun?

Such a din. This is supposed to be a peaceful trip. Just me and nature enjoying each other's company.

But, in the words of a silver screen time traveller, "They've found me. I don't know how. But they've found me".

Oh. It's just not on. Don't they know that a man's got to sleep? Don't they appreciate the quietness of this place? And why do they sound more like hair-lipped frogs than teenage tearaways? My God. What are they drinking?

Calm yourself Fennel. Breathe. Breathe. 1 – 2 – 3. Breathe again. Breeeethe…

Okay. I'm getting myself together now. I'm going to pause. Take stock of my surroundings. And listen to what's going on.

There. Did you hear it? That evil, invasive sound? Listen again. Very carefully. Do you hear?

Schliip, schliip, purrrp.

I ask you. What sort of a noise is that?

And again.

Schliip. Schliip. Schliip-schliip. Puurrrrrp…

And another, this time with an extra *pooouurrrp* that sounded like it had 'body'.

Oh. This is just too disgusting. These ruffians aren't even housetrained. Though if I'm going to confront them, it might as well be now, while they're preoccupied with another 'arrival'. This is it then. Fennel, brace yourself. Straighten your boxer shorts, pull your socks up above your knees and reverse your cap. It's time for action. Charge! Charge!! Charge!!!

Correction. First I'll see if I can undo the zip of my sleeping bag without making a noise, then unbutton the flap of the tent, just a little bit, so I can get half an eyeball's view of the opposition.

Okay. I've had a peek. There was nothing there. Nothing. Nothing whatsoever. No louts. No beer cans. Not even an oversized frog causing a commotion. I'm confused. There was definitely something there before. I heard it. We heard it. Right. I'm going out. I really am. Outside. Beyond this impenetrable fortress of taut canvas, into the dark of night. Farewell my friend. Sleep well in the knowledge that I set forth "to defend our island, whatever the cost may be."

Rustle. Snap.

"Eeeeuuwwoooouurrggghhhh!!!! Noooooooo. Noo. No!! Growoose. Urh. Urgh. Get off! Off!! Filthy, filthy, things!!"

Schwump. Schawump. Schump schwump. Shink. Shwink. Schump. Schaaaawump.

"I think that's done it. Yes. We're clear. No more of that nonsense. Not on my tent!"

Okay. I'm back with you now. Back inside the tent. Scribbling these notes while I try with my other hand to find the matches with which to light a candle. Ah. There they are. Matches in hand. One moment while I prepare some light.

Right. I can properly see to write now. Oh, good God. What's all this on my hands? It's slimy. Bear with me while I wipe them. Okay. That's done. Fennel. You did it. It's over.

I guess you're wondering what happened out there? What caused all the disturbance? Well I'll tell you. There were no louts. There was no frog. No lager cans or remains of a drunken party. There was. Well. Only. Slugs. *Damn dirty slugs!* Slithering all over the dewy surface of the tent, and all over each other. Doing things that I care not to think about. Writhing. Sinuously. Over and over. In a frothy mess that made the tent look like it was being shampooed. My poor, lovely, beautiful tent. My special place of comfort and warmth. Reduced to being a slug's squidge-blanket. And me, the innocent bystander; the first man in history to be accused of 'slugging'. Well I showed them who was boss. I soon broke up the orgy. Made more than the earth move for them, I'll tell ya. Oh yeah. Just call me the Sluginator. I swiped them clean off the tent with ninja-sharp karate chops and brutish flailing of arms. Off they flew, one by one, into the pitch black, feeling like they'd been nabbed by the father-in-law from hell for messing with his slug princess. They're gone now. That's for sure. They won't be coming back. Not while they know I'm around. Defender of the law that says "No sluggy-panky in the open after nightfall". And certainly not on my tent.

So. This is how it's going to be, this getting close to nature? A baptism of, er, well, I'd rather not think of it. Not the sort of immersion I'd planned. Though I'm sure it's something a cool shower would solve. There's rain on the horizon, so I'm keeping my (slightly sticky) fingers crossed for the heavens to open and purge this tent of its impurities. 'Snail trails' indeed!

So, it's time to snuff out the candle and attempt to sleep once again. A proper sleep this time. Without any disturbances. I bid you goodnight.

Ah. Silence. Alone once again in the wilds, without a care in the world.

Schliip. Schlip. Puuuurrrppp.

Oh, come on. Give me a break.

Right. Change of plan. I *am* going to sleep. But this time I'm going to dream of salt. Lots and lots of salt. Sprinkled all over this love-nest of a tent!

MAY

VI

NIGHT OF THE SILVER RAIN

Tonight I am experiencing the most beautiful and relaxing nocturnal scene. It's one of those events that remain in one's memory for a lifetime, a vision that forces us to stop whatever we're doing to just gaze in amazement. It makes me want to hold my hands aloft, with fingers outstretched, and look to the sky in the belief that I am in the presence of something celestial. Let me describe what I'm seeing and feeling.

I'm writing this journal at midnight, or thereabouts, on a night most unlike the one I experienced last month. I am sitting outside my tent, writing with clear view of my pen as it forms words on a page of molten silver. There is no orange candlelight or dazzling white from a Tilley lamp to illuminate the scene, just a glow that colours everything in a cool silver hue.

A full moon in the southeast creates this lucidity. It silhouettes the trees around me, which dapple shade onto the woodland floor. My encampment, in the clearing between the trees, is bathed in a pool of pearl light that gives everything here an ethereal glow. Even my tent, which by day is a dull olive green, has a pale grey sheen, making it appear dusted with frost.

A thin layer of cloud covers the sky, diffusing the

moonlight and creating a halo above the lake. The veil, which appears ready to drift to the ground like an empty parachute, moves gently on a high breeze. Below, the air is calm. There isn't a ripple on the surface of the lake or a rustle in the trees. In fact, the lack of breeze, combined with the tranquillity of this nocturnal hour, has hushed everything into almost catacomb quietness. The loudest things I can hear are the dull rasping of air passing through my nostrils and a something that sounds like eggshells being crushed between wet fingertips. (Upon inspection, this turns out to be the sound of my tongue moving in my mouth.) If I hold my breath and keep my body still, I can hear the faintest sound of pampas rustling in the distance. But there is no wind, and no tall grass. I listen harder. No. It's not the sound of dry grass. It is, I believe, the sound of a billion tiny raindrops entering the pool. A rain shower is moving up the valley and will soon reach these woods. I should head for cover, but with the light the way it is, I must go down to the lake to witness the spectacle.

I've walked as quietly as possible down through the trees to the lake's edge. Holding this notebook close to my chest, I am able to continue writing and not risk soaking the paper. Because, as I predicted, the rain has reached the wood. But it's falling so gently, as if the raindrops don't want to make a fuss. The clouds don't look heavy enough for rain, but I can see circular ripples forming and spreading, colliding into each other like a ballroom full of waltzing hula-hoopers. It makes me smile – the knowledge that I shall probably get soaked, yet I continue to enjoy every second of the drenching.

I've looked up from the water and back to the clouds, which now seem to have an inner glow as they pass in front of the moon. Strangely, even the raindrops have an optical radiance, as if they're emitting light from within; they emerge from the sky with the brightness of snow falling above a street lamp. It is a night of silver rain.

I should be feeling chilled by this moisture, but I'm not. The air is warm, unusually warm for May, and refreshing, like new bed linen. Perhaps, if I were at home, it might feel humid and stuffy. But not so here. Beneath the trees, the air has a 'thinness' that makes it delectable to breathe. With each breath I can taste the earthy scents of moist humus mixed with a floral scent of, hmm, what's that? Oh, yes, it's the smell of fish about to spawn. If you're not an angler then you might think that fish cannot be smelled through water, and even if there were such a smell, that it would be a vile 'fishy' scent. Well, let me assure you that it can be smelled and that it has a floral sweetness that reminds me of the perfume of a plant. The blooms of a Bleeding Heart plant, to be precise. At first I thought that the smell was of roach but, given its intensity, I'd stake that it is from carp, they being the roach's larger relative and the most boisterous of courters. (Think of a group of overweight men dressed in gold lamé tracksuits, suffering from too much alcohol, vying for the attention of the only girl in the nightclub.) The carp will be spawning soon but, I hope, not tonight. It is too peaceful, and the thought of golden-scaled fish leaping into the air (and contrasting with the silver scene above) does not appeal to me. Besides, it's only May, and carp aren't supposed to be in my thoughts for a month or more yet. If I desire a contrast to this heavenly scene then I shall think of fishing for sea trout on an inky black night when not even the bats leave their roosts. (Actually, thinking of bats, it's unusual not to see or hear any wildlife on such a bright night. Perhaps all the owls, badgers, foxes, deer and voles are sitting back in wonderment, marvelling at this splendid scene, just like me?)

I will retire to my tent at some point, to gaze up at the illuminated canvas and cherish this idyllic night, while knowing, sadly, that the moment won't last. Things will soon change. The moon will drift behind the pine trees in the west and a new day will dawn. And I expect company soon. The fishing season begins in a few weeks and the lake will no longer be my exclusive home. But I don't want to think about the future. Not at this special time. It is a moment that illustrates the importance of 'the moment', of just sitting, standing or lying down to look, listen and feel for all the subtleties that exist in quiet moments like this.

Through careful observation, and being alert at the right time, we can experience Nature at her best. And on nights like tonight, when everything is perfect, we can be bathed in the beauty of silver rain.

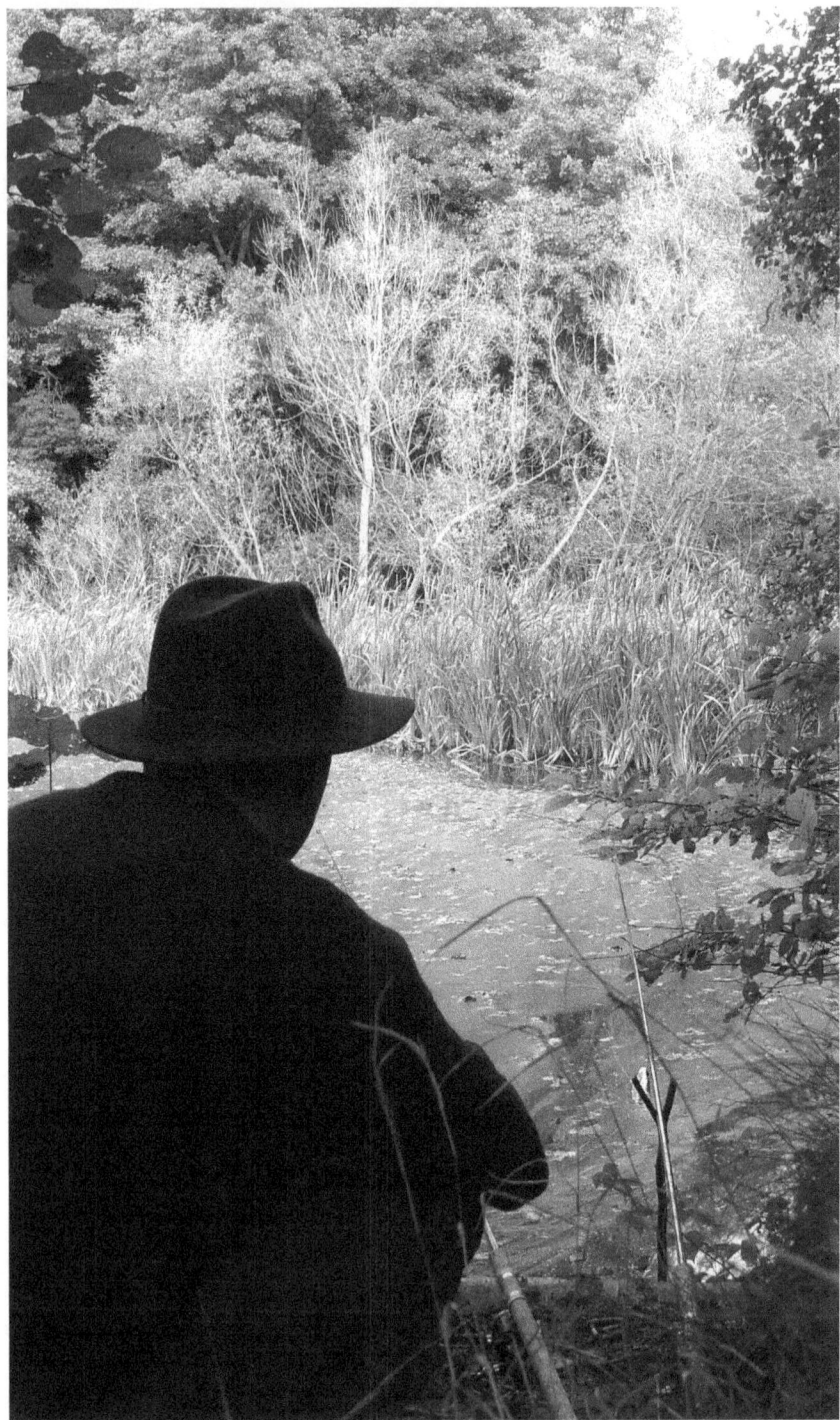

JUNE

VII

BACK TO THE FUTURE

"The Martians seem to have calculated their descent
with amazing subtlety – their mathematical learning
is evidently far in excess of ours."

H. G. Wells

Shhh! Keep quiet, or they might hear you. Who? The
invaders of course! Great metallic beasts that arrived
in the night, intent upon world domination and the
de-tweeding of anything organic. Stop! Look me in the
eyes and do as I say. "Stay still. And be calm!" Done it?
Good. Then I'll explain our situation.

I'm writing this cowering beneath a large
rhododendron bush. Its leaves are providing just
enough concealment for me and you to go unnoticed.
I settled into this spot last night, at dusk, as is tradition
for anglers about to begin the coarse fishing season. I'd
baited the water here for a number of days, feeding an
area six feet from the bank, just off the overhanging
rhodies and before a dense bed of hornwort. The tench
have been here most mornings for their breakfast, and
all was going to plan. A plan that saw me cast in at
midnight and then settle down onto a blanket to await

the first bite. I must have dozed off, because the next thing I remember is being startled awake by the crashing bombardment of an intergalactic invasion.

Not twenty feet from me is a mechanical creature with three metal legs that have apparently evolved to scuttle crablike across the frozen rock of some distant planet. It has four red eyes and four black spindly arms that point skywards, apparently in communication with some guiding mother ship. Behind the creature is a bulbous green craft that must have touched-down while I was asleep. Its landing has flattened all the vegetation within a twenty-foot radius; the clearing looks like a super-league crop circle. (I've concluded that it landed from above because, as I survey the scene in more detail, I can see that branches in the trees overhead are snapped and torn from their trunks.) There are five more of these invaders, each positioned with laser-beam accuracy at equidistant points around the lake. Fortunately, the creature nearest to me has not noticed my rod jutting out over the water, or the line meandering across the surface, or the porcupine quill sitting motionlessly next to the weed. The aliens are communicating with each other in a series of bleeps and peeps. They're evidently electrical, so I conclude that they must only be able to see things that conduct electricity. (They are blind to my wooden rod, nylon line and quill float. And judging by the damage around them, to the surrounding vegetation as well.) Nature haters? We know them too well: lifeless creatures created without emotion or aware of anything that is peripheral to their purpose.

Ooh. What's this? One of the creature's arms has just

lunged over, its fourth eye has started blinking furiously and it has – from somewhere I can't determine – released a nauseating banshee wail, like fingernails being run down a blackboard. The green craft shuddered and, with a smoker's cough, spat out what appears to be a fully-grown man. He stumbled to the ground as if reeling from an electric cattle prod, and then scrambled to get to the machine. Is he a prisoner of war, attempting to make his bid for freedom? He is not. He is a slave to his alien master, dutifully assisting the machine. He regained its posture and, as I can now see, is holding onto the creature's arm while it pulls a fish from the lake with the speed and tenderness of a retracting tape measure. He has now scooped the fish from the water. Oh. He's just cursed. Obviously his master wasn't pleased. He looks frustrated. He's walked past the green craft and walked towards a four-wheeled white craft. He opened a door in the side of the ship, climbed inside and then turned on an audio device to communicate with the other supreme beings at the lake. I heard one speak back to him, in a gruff tone that implied it too was displeased by his actions. (The lyrics to Pink Floyd's *Comfortably Numb* spring to mind…)

Now's our chance. With the alien creature and its slave separated, we can make our escape though the undergrowth and back to the safety of the wood. I've reeled in my line, gathered my things and am about to make a run for it. If you don't hear from me again then you'll know I've been caught in an attractor beam and forced into an existence of believing that romance is for girls and the world is as lifeless as cinder. Here goes…

Okay. I made it. And I'm glad to see that you made it too. I had to crawl 100 yards on my elbows and knees, and then run like a gazelle during a stampede, but I'm now out of sight of the invaders and able to slow my breathing to something approaching normal. The endangered species known as *Fennellum hudsonium* is safe once more, sheltering at the far end of the lake, not far from my tent and the cover of the woods.

Of course, the adrenaline I've just felt is more to do with my fertile imagination than the reality of a new War of the Worlds. I know that these Martians aren't here to take over our precious world (well, that's a separate debate). They have more focused plans. Their intention is simple: to remove the largest fish from the lake as efficiently and mechanically as possible, then put them back with equal speed, so that the process can be repeated. Again. And again. Until they get so bored that they sell all their gear and take up golf. Their human captors are brainwashed into thinking that the master race is absolute, that their way is the only way. But these Martians are merely modern anglers going about their business, using as much technology as possible to catch fish and distance themselves from the nature about them. As with so many modern developments, the creators and followers of this creed are more concerned with 'could' than 'should'. Which doesn't make me feel any safer. Compared to such lethal firepower, I am but a pathetic excuse of an angler. I would come under fire for my inability to catch a fish without smiling and for my inferior, inadequate and out-dated fishing tackle and dress. I am the weaker species and, wishing to live past lunchtime, have decided to hide away from all that bother. But I won't labour the point here. Instead, I've found a quiet, out of the way corner of the pool where I hope to be undisturbed for the remainder of the day. It's not the sort of place that would attract the Martians. It's too small for their landing craft and not expansive enough for their long-range missiles. But it's perfect for a lowly native like me. There's an attractive fringe of reedmace opposite that should hold some fish, and a silvery scum on the surface to provide cover. Actually, I can't believe that I didn't fish here earlier; but as with so many things in life, I'd convinced myself that things must be best at the place requiring the furthest walk. (Ironically, this has turned out to be true. The modern anglers fishing at the other end of the lake would never venture up here. It's too far from the track, too far for them to walk from their transit vans, too far into the unknown.)

That modern scene doesn't appeal. It's too urgent, too competitive, too 'butch'. Instead, I seek something altogether gentler and subtler. Somewhere like this quiet corner of a lake, where the afternoon shall consist of the lake, its wildlife, and us. Nothing more.

If the aliens represent the future of angling, then I am proud to have my back to the future.

JULY

VIII

CANEHENGE

The arrival of anglers at the lake has changed the dynamic of the pool. The waterfowl, which previously was active and loud, now seems subdued and cautious; even the fish are less evident than before. It is as if the lake is retiring from view, like a fox in a hedgerow when a hunt passes by. Also, I've found that my observations have become unhealthily focused on the activities of anglers. I'm more than curious. I'm downright nosy.

My fascination with the anglers ranges from how long it takes them to set up their mountains of gear, to how many baits they catapult into the water, and where they cast. My conclusions are 'too long,' 'too many,' and 'too close to me'. While I applaud them as brothers of the angle, I can't help but be repelled by their style of multi-rod, heavyweight angling. There's no place for competitiveness or urgency in angling. It's supposed to be a recreation, a switch-off from the grind of daily life. There's plenty enough stress in a working week already (says he who's spent the last four months enjoying a period of creative 'home working').

Actually, modern anglers aren't all bad. Some of them are quite cultured in their normal lives and can tell the difference between Sterling Artois and Cornershop Pils.

Some even have a sense of humour and can laugh at the absurdity of their actions. (And a few can see the tongue in my cheek when I'm talking about them.)

One of the anglers here has been in residence since the start of the season. That's three weeks and four days. He's been remarkably efficient during this time. His lines have been in the water throughout, and he's been outside of his bivouac no more than twice per day, for reasons other than answering the call of nature. I think he even caught a fish, once, though I can't be sure. Eventually, I had to introduce myself to him. It didn't go well. He made enough gestures for me to realise that I was intruding. I explained that I was living up in the wood and might be seen fishing from time to time. He gave me a saddened look then passed me an unopened tub of Pot Noodle as a farewell gift. (The offending 'Not Poodle' is now buried near to the camp, along with the infamous curried squirrel – which seemed like a good idea at the time but still insisted on climbing trees two days after I'd eaten it.)

I digress. I was supposed to be writing about, or recovering from, the arrival of so many modern anglers at the lake. Not recounting the story of Squirreldaloo.

Back to more serious matters: Modern Angling. Being confronted head-on by the cold and contorted face of the modern angling scene made me yearn to be far away from the bleeping of bite 'deceivers' and humming of plastic bait boats (that chug through the water like a constipated otter).

I am a man of the fly and float, of bamboo rods, simple baits and a desire to get as close as possible to the

fish I intend to catch. Sadly, there was a time a few years back when I distanced myself from this sentimental style of fishing and 'tooled-up' to fish with the aliens. It was a mistake. I wasn't in a happy place, and wasn't thinking straight. Which is why it didn't last and why I now keep my distance from the serious and ambitious side of angling. This 'dark side', as my friends call it, is never far away. Some of my acquaintances have been deceived by its curse, lost forever into the darkened recesses of nylon domes. They cut their hair short, as if for military action, and begin talking in numbers rather than words. Alas, they have all drowned in the festering cauldron that boils chemically enhanced baits and sterilises the very soul of angling.

Fishing simply, with split cane rods and antique fishing tackle, is a deliberate, conscious, purposeful decision to steer away from the seedier side of angling.

I fish in this basic way to compensate for the blackened side of the sport. Doing so, for me at least, shines a strong light on the beauty and art of angling. It is this brighter side, the romantic side, the emotional side, that appeals to me. It's the side where grown men will be found hugging each other in the knowledge that they will be going fishing together.

My time here in the woods has enabled me to think about the future of this peculiar 'traditional' branch of angling. I knew that turning my back on the modern angling scene was the right thing to do. I knew that I had to hide away and seek undisturbed fishing. But how? Perhaps I should only fish during the week when lakes and rivers are quieter? Or just at night, when I would be less aware of the presence of other anglers? And then I had an idea. Something much more grandiose. Something that's kept me awake at night in the knowledge that it could one day be real. An idea where we, and anglers like us, wouldn't have to retreat or hide. I'm talking about a lake dedicated to, and the exclusive preserve of, traditional angling.

Canehenge, as I've named it, would be set in a remote place where inner and outer calm could be found away from the warzone of competition or specimen angling. Only people with a relaxed, uncompetitive, 'Waltonian' spirit would find their way to the pool. If they chose to visit, then they would only wear traditional dress; if they chose to fish, then they would only use vintage tackle and traditional tactics. Wicker creels would creak, centrepin reels would 'crawk' and the plumes from Kelly Kettles would crown the pool in a halo of wood smoke.

Like-minded traditionalists would gravitate towards this angling ideal, to contentedly fish, read, relax and sleep while the rest of the angling world would look on, thinking the whole thing to be an eccentric, self-indulgent whim of the pompous elite.

And why not? Self-indulgence has always appealed to me. Why not spoil ourselves once in a while? Anything that is exclusive will be accused of elitism; living one's dreams will be called pretentious. So let's indulge the whim and see where it takes us.

It strikes me that traditional and modern anglers are heading the same way as Victorian game and coarse anglers. One has an elongated nose, down which he makes contemptuous looks towards the lesser man, who knows not the supreme pleasures of the purist. The other looks back with the smug knowledge that he has a bag full of fish. If this is true (I fear it is) then 'never the twain shall meet'. Give them separate places to fish, as happens today with fly and bait fishers. Let each do what they want to do, so long as they don't get under each other's feet. If two children don't enjoy the same game, then don't make them play together. Give them separate toys and plenty of space and both will be happy.

Canehenge, therefore, would be a bastion, a preserve for traditional angling, kept separate from developments occurring elsewhere in the angling world. Anglers would be strictly vetted to ensure the correct spirit, dynamic and 'poetry' of the membership. Or, as my friend Prof would say, "To keep the buggers out!"

Visiting Canehenge would be like going back in time, while having the secure knowledge that the 'henge was alive and well today, and an investment for the future. The angling conducted there would be an idealised, purist pursuit. 'Of and for traditionalists.' There wouldn't be many rules. If an angler stepped out of line, they would wake to find their boots filled with marmalade and their rods painted black. And so the bleeping of electric bite alarms would never be heard, green bivouacs would never pop up like a cluster of infected blisters, and bait boats would never be seen. Instead, everyone would use wooden rods, dress in tweed and sleep beneath canvas tents. Cars would be parked a mile away and vintage bicycles would be provided for anglers to cycle to the lakeside. Isolation and tranquillity would prevail and escapism would be guaranteed. Then, when you thought it couldn't get any better, Mr Crabtree would tap you on the shoulder and offer you a cup of tea.

It's an idealised dream, of course. But it could very easily materialise. Indeed, I wonder if such a pool already exists? Or should I say 'such a syndicate', as this is what would be required to create such a place. This is why I've focused, so far, on the anglers and their activities. But Canehenge has the potential to be more than this. I wonder whether it represents the potential to secure or develop a famous fishery? Maybe, maybe not. Developing a relatively unknown pool would be more likely, evolving it (if required) to meet the quirky tastes of traditionalists, and building its reputation among anglers.

A good starting point would be to find a lake that's very overgrown, in a state of neglect that implies no recent access to the pool and, consequently, a heightened sense of mystery. Mature trees would give the pool a sense of grandeur and age. If possible, the lake should be heavily weeded and rich with wildlife. If the pool contains fish, then that's great but not essential. I like the thought of seeding a pool with an historic strain of fish – probably wild carp – and then protecting the water from any future fish imports that could 'soil' the purity of the existing stock. Finally, the lake would need historical connections. Not necessarily an angling-related history, merely an association with a historic building, folly or landmark – something that has provenance and enough to give the lake some lineage and added meaning.

This is my dream: a mature and historic lake, fished only by traditional anglers using vintage-style tackle; where we may spend our time in blissful ignorance of the modern world, and catch considerably more than fish.

Remember the name: Canehenge. A place of exaltation, somewhere to raise our cupped hands to the sky and drink from the well of contentment. Somewhere to stand proud. And be as one. Provided, of course, moths don't get at our tweeds and woodworm doesn't eat our rods.

IX

AFLOAT IN A PUNT

The lake today seems bigger, brighter, and more expansive. I can see blue skies and a dazzling sun framed by cumulous cloud. In my peripheral vision I can just make out a ring of treetops and a cloud of dust rising from behind a combine harvester that rattles across a nearby field. This unique view of the pool is formed because I am lying face up on the floor of an old wooden punt. A punt that is drifting ever so slowly across the pool. I can hear water lapping against its sides, but I cannot see it. The dark, aged timbers of the punt serve as blinkers that force my sight upwards to the sky.

I've been lying here for about two hours. It may be longer. Time isn't important. I'm enjoying a spontaneous moment that has no purpose other than to let my body and mind drift in an idle and dreamy state. Corporate folk might suggest that I'm being lazy, that I should have something more productive to do with my afternoon. But resting here 'doing nothing' seems the right thing to do on such a beautiful summer's day. The act is as rewarding as its apparent pointlessness.

Actually, my being in the punt did at first have purpose. I boarded it to fish for roach, which I'd seen dimpling the surface at the centre of the pool. (At least that was my excuse when I skipped breakfast in favour of a paddle about the lake.) And I did fish, for a while, catching eight roach on fly-tackle before the mist rolled from the water and the sun rose into the sky. As the day grew hotter, I opted to ignore the shade beneath the trees and lie here, sweltering in nothing but yesterday's undies, lying on the boards of the punt, drifting to wherever the air currents took me. After being still for so long, I am incapable of moving quicker than ivy growing over a rock.

Lying in the punt, and drifting so slowly, gives me a feeling of weightlessness, as if I am floating not on water but in mid-air, held as if between two opposing magnetic fields. But there is no opposition here, and no conflict. I am alone once more at the lake. The last of the anglers has departed, bored, I guess, with the lack of carp activity during this minor heat wave. Or, as I'm now beginning to think, that he ran out of petrol for his electric generator. (Oh how I won't miss the constant 'tat-tat-tat-tat-tat' from the generator and the 'dum-dum-dum-dum-duddy-dadudum' from his portable television at 8pm each weeknight.)

I've been living a secretive life for too long, staying out of the way of people and doing my best to maintain a solitary existence (other than for Mrs H-to-Be's visits, of course). I doubt whether any of the anglers, other than Mr Pot Noodle, knew I was here. And so I am making the most of having the lake to myself again by idling in the punt and cooking like a sausage on a barbecue.

There are times in one's life when it is best to

stay hidden from view, moments that should not be disturbed, else the magic is lost. This is one of them. I am reassuringly hidden, so it needn't matter if the anglers were here. A passer-by would conclude that the punt had broken free of its moorings and was drifting like the Mary Celeste towards a distant shore. So there will be no disturbances for me. I am free to idle my time gazing at the blue skies and spotting faces in the clouds. (I've seen a convincing Winston Churchill and a cloud that looked like a fat woman poking her tongue through a Polo mint. One cloud reminded me of a well-risen Yorkshire pudding, while another looked like a well-filled bra. Maybe I've been alone for too long, or that these are signs that I will one day be served Sunday lunch by a waitress with an ample bosom and a face for radio?)

A flock of racing pigeons has just hurtled overhead, startling my vision into a sharper, less dreamier focus. (That buxom cloud has just burst in two. My mind boggles…)

There is something eternally satisfying about lying motionless for hours on end, watching the world move around us like the shadow on a sundial. I think back to my childhood and all those 'misspent' hours lying in the grass looking up at the sky, imagining that the swifts tumbling overhead were Spitfires engaged in aerial dogfight, and thinking that the whole world was way too spectacular for my young mind to comprehend. Then came the time when the angle of my neck straightened and it was no longer acceptable to spend the day gazing up at the sky, or doing anything reminiscent of child-like dreaming. Yet throughout history people have gazed at the skies in wonder. You only have to stand at the base of a church steeple to understand why.

Those who prefer to stare at the ground, checking their shoes or kicking their heels, sadden me and make me want to turn the floor into a giant mirror. Their focus is so much closer, their vision smaller and less interesting. Whether by choice or circumstance, they exist in a closeted world. Some may have purposeful strides, but they see little of their journey. "Stop and unplug," say I; "look around you, at the vastness and greatness of the natural world." Some stop. Others need binoculars to tie their shoelaces.

Enough observations. What's here and now is important. This hot afternoon in August, that might see me dive from the punt and swim to shore, is here for a purpose. To teach me that doing nothing can be as rewarding as doing something. And doing very little can be as productive, in a creative sense, as doing a lot.

Which makes me realise that I'm too comfortable to go for that swim. I'm in no hurry to do anything. I'll probably lie here for the rest of the day. (Great term, that, 'rest of the day'.) My stomach hasn't started rumbling yet and I have no desire to return to the tent. But wait a minute. There's a cloud over there that looks like a baby's bottom. If it rains, I'm off!

SEPTEMBER

X

THE LAST CARP OF SUMMER

The sunburn I developed back in August (as a result of spending the whole day drifting in the punt) has finally eased to a point where I can wear more than my pride, and shun my reputation as the Human Lobster. Like a snake on a rock, I have shed my skin and grown another. I feel reborn and ready to resume activities.

Today I am going fishing. The wild carp of the lake are showing on the shallows. They are feeding, I think, on the bloodworms that live in the mud beneath the water. The fish are readying themselves for another winter's torpor, and are filling their bellies while they have the chance. I have some lobworms (collected last night from the dewy grass in the field next to the lake), so I'm optimistic about catching my favourite type of fish. I'm going to grab a rod and net, and see what destiny will bring.

Okay. I'm in position now, kneeling behind a small alder that grows from the water's edge. The lake here is about thirty yards wide and about three feet deep. The far bank is a tangled mass of fallen trees and brambles; the nearside bank is steep, with overhanging oak and beech trees. I can see two shoals of carp, each containing five fish. Each fish is about the size and shape of a magnum of champagne (or, in modern angler speak, about the size of two bivvy slippers placed heel to heel) – too small to warrant the attentions of specimen hunters, but ideal for pleasure anglers like me who know that size isn't nearly as important as beauty. Some fish are just basking in the sun; others are swimming, swirling and flashing in the water, sending up vortices and leaving great clouds of silt behind them.

The fish are out of range at the moment, at least for my freelined lobworm, which is useless at front crawl. (I made a point of only bringing basic tackle with me – no float or weights for casting, only an eight-foot bamboo rod, a centrepin reel, sixty yards of line, a packet of hooks, a net and a pocketful of worms.) So, no hurry. I'll sit here and watch the fish, waiting for one to swim within casting range, which I estimate to be no more than ten feet from the bank.

The water at this corner of the lake is much calmer than down near the dam, which is being brushed by gusts of wind and is glinting in the sunshine. The water here has a silvery scum line along the margin by my feet and, further out, has a distinctly green, murky look. I'm pleased that the water still has its summer colour. All too soon, the water temperature will drop, fish activity will lessen and the water will take on a slightly sterile clarity, one that longs for the wriggle of grubs and fanning of fins. But the water now has movement. If I stare at it for long enough I can see that it is subtly swaying. Leaves floating on the surface move in and out, as if resting on Poseidon's sleeping chest, and, when I take my gaze from the water and focus on the trees above, I notice that my eyes have adopted this gentle rocking motion too, as the leaves and branches seem to pulse in and out. I believe I'm being hypnotised by the pool.

Shake your head Fennel. You're supposed to be fishing.

I remember reading in Bernard Venables' *Angler's Companion* that those who make serious attempts to catch carp usually fall under a spell and find its effect upon them hypnotic. Worryingly, he also wrote that carp cannot be approached in a casual way. Which rules out any chance of me catching today.

I am not a serious angler; I'm altogether casual in my fishing. After my ordeal a few years ago, I'm determined to embrace the sedentary nature of carp fishing. The carp will swim closer, of that I am sure. In the meantime I shall be content to sit and dream, letting the hours accumulate with graceful inevitability, like mist settling in a valley.

Although technically still summer, today seems decidedly autumnal. The season is changing. The days are growing shorter, the nights are colder (my ceramic hot water bottle has been requested from home) and each dawn grows heavier with dew. Hazelnuts hang plump in the woodland coppice and the recent lack of rain has started the premature bronzing of leaves. Soon they will be dressed in their autumn colours and the landscape will be washed in crimson, gold and copper.

I'm excited by the prospect of autumn. There's never any regret in losing a season because the one that follows brings with it so much natural beauty and traditions. I'm joyful in the knowledge of an imminent conker season, of drifts of leaves and, of course, the autumn harvest. The blackberry crop this year is superb. They've not suffered from mildew or been gorged upon by blackbirds, so bumper pickings will be had. (Mmm. Blackberry and apple crumble, blackberry jam on toast, blackberry conserve with rice pudding. Blackberry liqueur. Delicious.)

I digress. Again. You must be wondering where the fish are. Actually, so am I. Oh, there they are. They've moved from the far bank and are now circling about in the centre, looking for another feast of midge larvae.

This really is lazy fishing (not that I've cast in yet). It's so different to spinning for pike or casting a fly to trout, which in comparison seems more frantic, and less contemplative. Which is why traditional carp fishing – away from all the gizmos and gadgetry of the modern scene – is such a simple and leisurely recreation. But with all this time waiting for 'the chance', I find that my mind is busy searching for things to do. During a normal day, at home, I would be actively making job lists or starting projects, but this place lacks the reminders of 'urgent tedium'. My mind is free to dream and reflect.

I've been here for six months and have found most of what I sought. But I know that, even regarding fishing, I'm craving new scenery.

As I wait for the carp to swim nearer, I can't help but think of future adventures. Salmon fishing in Scotland, pike fishing in Ireland, and wild brown trout in Wales. But they'll have to get in line behind the non-fishing activities that are equally, if not more, important. Like moving house and planting my new garden, a walking holiday with Mrs H (we're getting married next week), and finally doing something with all the writing notes I've built up over the years. But, as I look lakewards again, I know that all of these dreams will have to wait. The carp have finally come to within casting range.

I've just cast my lobworm into the lake. An underarm swing was enough to flick the worm on the end of the line to within six feet of a feeding carp. I saw the worm sink slowly into the depths, wriggling with displeasure at its enforced morning wash.

The line has settled in an arc beneath the rod tip

and I'm waiting for it to tighten. I can't see the worm any more, as the fish are swimming all around it and muddying the water.

Ooh. Hang on. Already? So soon? There! There! It's pulling tight. Stri-

Nothing. I flicked the rod upwards, expecting to set the hook and see a bow wave appear in the water as a carp fled for freedom, but I connected with nothing other than an oak branch overhead (which has grabbed hold of my hook and line and won't give it back). The carp were unfazed by the sight of a worm swimming at ten feet per second past their gills. They just carried on feeding. Now, alas, they are cruising off again. Out into the lake while I will have to climb the tree to retrieve my hook. I fear that we have missed our chance. Those fish, the last carp of summer, will remain uncaught.

I have no desire to continue fishing. I could get all keen and cast again, or go in search of carp elsewhere. But I don't want to. I had my chance and feel no urgency to prove myself. After all, who is there to impress? There's only you and me here. And we know that catching fish is just an incidental pleasure of a day spent beside water. I promise you, though, that we will have a proper wild carp adventure soon. One that will fill a Journal of its own. But not just yet. First we should retire to our woodland camp and mark the end of summer. A cup of tea, perhaps, and a toast to 'that which once was'. (And which, if we hold on to the dream, may 'be' once more.)

XI

THE MACFENNEL CHALLENGE

When I arrived at the lake I wasn't 'travelling light', as I'd foolishly believed, but was in fact beginning a camping trip more akin to a weekend's stay at Butlins. I'd bought enough food with me to last a month and enough loo roll for my entire stay. Eight months in the woods have hardened me, or at least firmed up my beliefs that if a man's going to fend for himself, then he needs to leave his credit card at home.

I've always prided myself as being a proper camper. What suburbanites would now call a 'wild camper'. The thought of going camping on nicely level mown grass, with access to a shop, a bar, shower block, toilets, swimming pool and launderette? No. That's not my style at all. I'd rather camp it out in my back garden. So what must you have thought, back in March, when reading about my over-cautious supplies? Not good Mr Fennel. People will talk. It's time to dust off my tinderbox, whittle myself a spear, add some camouflage paint to my face and reclaim my reputation as a properly wild camper. Just bear with me while I apply some hand cream.

The challenge that I'm going to set myself is similar to what huntsmen would call a MacNab, except that

I'm not going to catch a salmon and shoot a stag all in the same day. I have a smaller challenge, but in a shorter timeframe. I'm going to call it a MacFennel. (In case you're wondering, the answer is 'Yes, it does involve fast food, just not from that awful burger chain'.) I will catch a pike, 'stalk' a rabbit, forage a mixed punnet of nuts, berries and mushrooms, and use these ingredients to cook a three-course meal. All within five hours. If I fail, I will ceremoniously eat the buried Pot Noodle given to me by that bivvy angler in June. So. I have a challenge. A reward of renewed credibility, and a potential punishment of weeklong indigestion. Five hours to succeed. From now. Okay Fennel, stop writing and Go! Go!! Go!!!

Hmm. I forgot that the kettle was about to boil. I'll start in about twenty minutes.

During my time by the lake I've eaten all manner of wild food. I started with trout from the local stream, lightly fried in butter, and then progressed to pike, which I've found to be bland but 'edible'. (Perch, on the other hand, are the nicest fish I've ever tasted.) I'm hungry, so my pike will be hunted with stomach-rumbling urgency, by casting a spinner towards the reeds in the corner of the lake nearest to the camp.

Rabbits are plentiful hereabouts and are usually found in the field next to the wood. I've hunted and eaten rabbits most weeks, so they won't be a problem to find, or dispatch with the air rifle (though they might not make the best eating within hours of killing). There are plenty of hazelnuts in the coppice behind me, and Spanish chestnuts further up in the wood.

Blackberries seem to be growing everywhere right now, and there are some hedgehog mushrooms growing near to the beech stump by the tent. I've got it covered. Best have that cup of tea.

Of course, I could have some fun by swapping things around – climbing a tree and hooking a rabbit with rod and line, or shooting a pike with the air rifle. But no. That's just stupid, and about as sporting as attaching one's fishing bait to a 3oz lead weight. I'll stick to my original plan and deploy it with all the confidence of a man who's dined on fried fish and rabbit casserole for half the year.

So while I'm sipping this tea, I will make a quick plan: First, I'll get the fire started. Second, I'll get some water boiling and drop in a selection of wild herbs (I'll go for garlic, wood sorrel and bittercress) followed by some potatoes 'acquired' from a neighbouring field. Third, I'll grab the air rifle, run to the edge of the wood and, all being well, bag myself a rabbit. Fourth, I'll bring the rabbit back to the camp, skin and gut it, then pop it in the saucepan of boiling water. Fifth, I'll head down to the lake, catch a pike, come back up to the camp, fillet it, and leave it resting while I go foraging. Sixth, I will collect the blackberries from the hedgerow by the potato field, get hazelnuts from the coppice at the edge of the wood, chestnuts from the tree next to the badger sett in the wood, and then return back to the camp, to collect the mushrooms. Seventh, the mushrooms will go into the casserole, along with the peeled nuts. Phew. I feel tired just writing about it.

The food won't be restaurant quality, and not my

go-to fried egg sarnies, but it will fill a gap. In case you're wondering, the dress code for the meal is 'informal'. Feel free to bring a bottle of something good and, as I don't have any, a bottle opener and some glasses. (I'm reminded of the W. C. Fields quote, "…of my safari in Africa. Somebody forgot the corkscrew and for several days we had to live on nothing but food and water".) Tell your other half that you shall be dining out (literally) on a meal of "Pike fillet pan-fried in garlic butter; rabbit casserole with mushrooms, potatoes and chestnuts; followed by 'an arrangement' of wild berries". Oh, and an urgent trip to the bushes.

Okay. Enough talking. Time to put the plan into action. I will depart, returning – I hope – with the ingredients for tonight's meal, and making a few notes as I go. Right. See you shortly.

Progress reports:

Fire. Success. A toasty furnace blazing away.

Water. Success. Though the stock looks insipid.

Rabbit. Success. Sort of. Took a while as the little blighters stayed just out of range and, after eight months without a proper bath, there was no such thing as a 'downwind approach'.

Nuts. Well, enough said. I managed to scavenge a few that hadn't been gnawed by the squirrel. Chestnuts were easier to find, though de-husking them was like thumb-wresting a hedgehog. Blackberries were easy. They are the floozies of the hedgerow.

Pike. Success, in many small parts. There are hundreds of them in the lake. My challenge was catching one large enough to fillet. After an hour or so, I was able to catch a fish of twenty-one-and-a-quarter pounds that will make a fine starter for tonight's meal. What d'you reckon? A fillet each? Only joking. I could never take such a fish. I have a four-pound pike for the pan.

Mushrooms. In the bag. They were always going to be the easy task. Trickier at other times of year, but not today.

Job done. I'm now back at camp, catching my breath and feeling rather smug at my achievements. I still have another half-hour to go before the deadline and can reflect upon the first MacFennel challenge. The rabbit was by far the hardest part. But as I pulled the trigger, saw the 'poof' of fur and the rabbit leap into the air, then bowl over and land with a thud, I knew I had proved myself a master hunter. Lord of the Bright Eyes.

Just don't tell the Anti's.

I'm gazing at the rabbit now; its rear legs are poking out from the top of the casserole pot in most undignified fashion. Poor thing. Its destiny is a rather dodgy stew comprising of some stolen potatoes and not nearly enough seasoning. Hmm. Actually, that casserole pot doesn't look right. There's no steam coming from it.

Oh damn and bunnied hoppery! The fire has gone out. I've just investigated the pot and the stock is tepid and coated with waxy scum. It looks about as appetising and undercooked as Alaskan road kill. There's not nearly enough time to get cooking again. Fennel has failed his own MacFennel challenge. I am the hunting Eunuch, forced to eat a stale Pot Noodle and a side dish of humble pie.

Oh, what am I talking about? There's no such thing as 'not enough time'. I don't even have a watch. Time is my own, categorised as nothing more than 'morning, afternoon, evening and night'. Well, it's still light enough to see, so I'll get the fire started again and keep going.

Our meal's going to end up as a late-night candlelit supper. Which is probably for the best. I've seen what it looks like.

XII

A GIFT OF LIFE

It is nearly time to leave the lake. Tonight is my final night here. Mrs H arrives in the morning to take me back home, which I now know to be a very special place indeed.

I'm missing my wife and our home, and crave the luxury of a soft bed and a hot bath. Conditions at the lake are telling me it's right to depart. There have been several hard frosts this week that have kept me shivering in my tent for longer than is healthy. I've raided all of the firewood within an easy walk of the camp and no matter how long I air my clothes in the sun, I just can't get the dampness out. My joints are stiff and I'm finding that holding a pen is causing my hand to lock tight with cramp. I have to prise each finger open and then warm my hands on a mug of tea. So you'll excuse me when I tell you that I'm writing this journal from the warmth of my sleeping bag and the shelter of the tent, even though the sun is at its peak in the sky and my early morning fire has smouldered to ash.

When I set out on this adventure, I planned to write about what I saw and felt. And then, on my final day, I would write a moving and meaningful piece in honour of my time beside the lake. Now that I have reached the

end of the journey, I know that I don't have to write such a conclusion. All of my writing this year has, either deliberately or accidentally, been an honest and fitting tribute to the lake. However, in case you've any doubts, I'm happy to say that my time here has been nothing short of life changing.

I've lived a very simple existence these past months. Sounds simple, doesn't it, this notion of simplicity? Simple things done simply by a simple person. But it's not as simple as it seems. Usually there are too many external forces trying complicate things. Too many conflicting views create a mesh of complexity that cocoons the original, brilliant, simple idea. Every layer of complexity creates greater distance from life's simple truths. The simple truth that I've discovered this year is that, although groups of people are good at making things happen, the greatest moments of creativity come in absolute solitude, when one's mind is free from distraction and able to probe the depths of the impossible.

I've written some whacky stuff this year. Most of which is kept in reserve for future projects. I've shared the bite-sized pieces with you here (these journals being the abridged version of an eventful year). But I've written so much more. This place has moved me to write about situations that I'd not considered possible. (Ever been in a Mexican standoff with two posturing cock pheasants? Trust me, when they attack, protect your eyes and run like hell.) My time in the wilds has given me the opportunity to get my head decidedly unstraight. I now know that individuality and creativity are slowly dampened by a normal job with normal people.

Now is not the time to write something sentimental. What I will do, however, is tell you about how I've shown my gratitude to the lake and its owner.

Do you remember me mentioning at the start of the year that the landowner granted me permission to camp here in return for working on his farm every Saturday? Well I have honoured this agreement, rolling up my sleeves every weekend since March, and undertaking all manner of menial estate tasks. I've repaired fencing, chopped logs, mown meadows, cleared culverts, shovelled manure, strimmed verges, and burned rubbish. I can proudly say that this work has been consistently enjoyable. But all this was expected of me. My time at the lake has delivered way more than I could have hoped for, so I felt the need to do something extra to give appropriate thanks. So, in agreement with the landowner and syndicate leader, I've been spending an hour or two each week doing what I can to enhance the lake and its immediate surroundings.

When a group of individuals takes control of something, they ultimately (often immediately) make changes to it so that it suits their tastes or needs. They feel compelled to make their stamp. (Ever moved into a house and felt the urge to get the paint rollers out before you've unpacked?) Successive syndicates have held the fishing rights to this pool and it's evident that each has tampered with the lake's surroundings. Like removing the shrubby undergrowth from the western end of the pool, strimming clear the wild flowers from along the dam, erecting fishing platforms made from leftover timber, and snapping branches from trees to allow for easier casting. Most of all, I noticed how the bird life was less evident by the lake than further back in the wood, and how the owls were vocal in spring but progressively less so through the year.

My intention was to wipe clean the footprints left by others, restoring the lake to how it had been, or would have become, without the meddling of successive generations of angling work parties. I also decided to give the bird life in the immediate area a boost. Therefore, I am delighted to announce (from the cosiness of my sleeping bag) that this year I have grown and planted several hundred trees and shrubs; made and erected four-dozen bird boxes (including some large contraptions for the owl family); systematically cleared all litter from around the lake and dismantled any derelict fishing platforms.

My delight comes not from giving back to nature today but from thoughts of how these gifts will grow and be of greater benefit in the future. A heeled-in sapling might not look much today (and could get nibbled by rabbits or deer tomorrow) but in fifty or sixty years? I doubt I'll be around to see it, but I'd expect the tree to be a mature and stately reminder of someone who was very appreciative of his time by the lake. All I really want is for our world to become increasingly more beautiful. Mine is a gift of life. Which is, after all, what the lake has given to me.

Using my gardening skills was the obvious thing to do. I hope that these words will also be a suitable tribute. But enough sentiment. It's nearly time for me to pack away the last non-essential things into my rucksack. The remainder of the day will be a private time, with me taking a final stroll around the lake and then enjoying a special dinner at nightfall. (I'm going to cook jacket potatoes in the campfire.) Dismantling this tent in the morning will be a sombre event. Not that I'm sad to leave, but it will feel like waving goodbye to a good friend.

This waterside scene, this wood, and this tent, are a little piece of rural England that I'm proud to have called home.

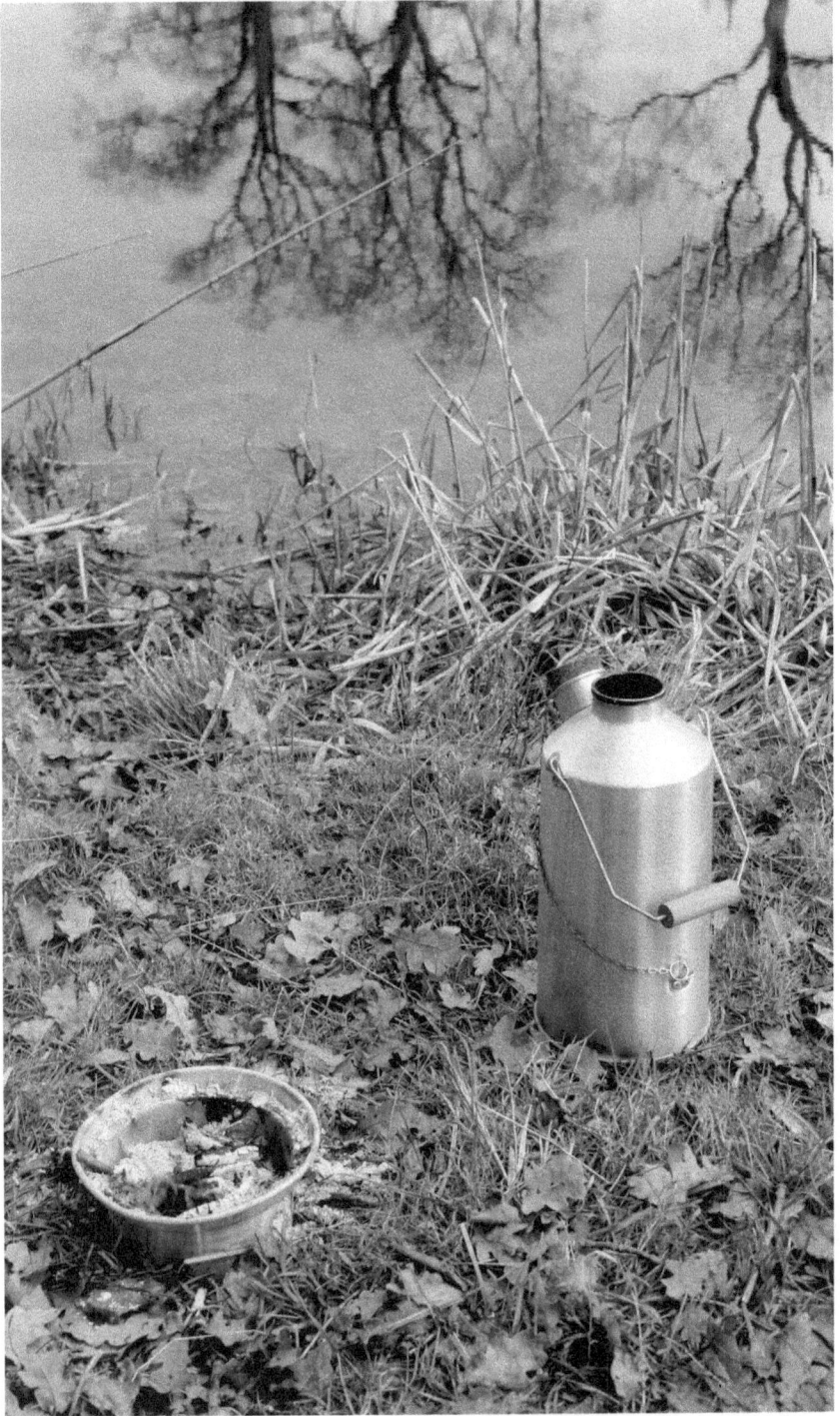

XIII

FREEDOM WITHIN

The Ancient Greek historian Thucydides wrote, "The secret of happiness is freedom. The secret of freedom is courage". I'm sure you'll agree that I was courageous in confronting those amorous slugs back in April, but did it make me happy? It did not. They might have been practising free love, but such freedom was too much, too soon, for me. I stayed in my tent for the remainder of the night, trying my best to ignore the 'wild life' around me.

I was reminded of Thucydides' words this evening, as I sat beside the campfire, enjoying the finest jacket potato I've ever tasted. (When baked in clay, the shell is tapped free and then the skin of the potato can be cracked open. Steam rises and the lightest, fluffiest, potato inner is revealed. A knob of butter and a little salt, and I'm in heaven.)

As I ate the potato, and reflected upon my time at the lake, I became aware that my thoughts had drifted into daydream. I was imagining that I was at home with Mrs H, sitting in my favourite chair, reading a book about life in the woods. In the vision, I was escaping into a story where I was at a place just like this. The image developed and became clearer in my mind.

And then, as the fire crackled, I snapped out of my daze. I was dumbfounded. Why would an imagined vision of woodland life appear more enchanting than the real scene before me? Is the promise of adventure more exciting than the adventure itself? That standing atop a mountain, for example, is an anti-climax when compared to the excitement of beginning the climb? Or that living alone in a wood is not as free as the thought of escaping the confinement of four walls and an uninspiring job? I escaped all that back in March. So why do I still feel the need to escape?

You must be thinking, "What's Fennel got to worry about? He's been swanning about that lake for the past three months, enjoying the quiet life, while I've had all manner of troubles and chores to see to". And you'd be right. I've had it easy. I've felt the stress of work and modern life fall from my bones; my energy levels are higher than they've been since my teenage years. I've climbed trees, swum in the lake, rocked in a hammock, and done everything and anything I wanted, whenever I chose to do it. I've indulged all my escapist dreams. I'm here, away from everyone, living it up. Being a selfish and antisocial git. And loving every second. But I can't help feeling that I've taken the easy option. That there's a tougher, but more rewarding, adventure to be had.

Leaving the rat race is easy. All you have to do is quit your job, sell your house, and go and live in a tent in the middle of nowhere. It's *staying* out of the rat race that's tricky. I'm living in a tent, and yet don't feel especially free. Maybe the dream of being here was better than the reality? No, that's rubbish. I'm having a great time.

It's just that now I've been here for so long, I'm finding that my dreams are of other places. I'm like the traveller who says, "Thanks for the stop-off at the oasis; grateful for the drink, but gotta press on; there's a horizon over there with my name on it." The desire for discovery is too great; the image of greener grass too alluring. I keep on dreaming, but to find freedom, one must first search inwards. You'll never find yourself anywhere other than where you are right now.

Thucydides was right. My being here is not courageous. It's those who stay in or out of the system, and treasure their short but quiet moments of escape, who are truly free. They're the brave ones, the warriors who, in their daily endurances, shout "Freedom!" Because freedom is not a place. It's a state of mind.

It was French author and Nobel Prize winner André Gide who said, "Be faithful to that which exists within yourself". If you have burning desire to be free (as I have) you must first find this freedom within you. And to be free in this manner, you have to be comfortable with who and what you are. (It's not possible to run away from yourself. Unless, of course, you're schizophrenic and can take holidays outside your mind.)

If I have learned one thing this year it's that time alone helps us to remember who we are. There aren't the external pressures, fashions, and fads corralling us into being someone we're not. We're just 'us', with time on our hands to reveal, or decide, the person we want to be.

I spent too many years of my life living as someone else. Trying to be something I'm not. It resulted in darkness and confusion, where I couldn't remember my own name. My awakening last year, and my current existence in the woods, has helped me to rediscover myself, and find my freedom within.

Wouldn't it be great to be oneself all of the time? No cowering or hiding; just an honest representation of the person within. If it sounds like a big ask, then surround yourself with things that remind you of who you are. They'll give you courage and help to communicate your identity. This is my plan for when I return to the normal world, when I'll need to cling to something that reminds me of my time by the lake, and keeps me alive.

Freedom within is embodied in things as well as people. Like coins tossed into a wishing well, they contain our hopes and dreams. Take my rucksack for example. It's been with me throughout my lakeside adventure. It's my companion, into which I place my soul for safekeeping. It bears the scuffs and grime of many quests, each mark proving that dreams can become real. It takes me to exciting and unexpected places, for in its pocket is a compass but no map. There's never been a map. Only a compass whose dial always knows where it's pointing. It leads me forward. And the bag follows. Both rucksack and compass promise great adventures, because they have the spirit, and freedom, within.

That's my message, then, as the night closes in on our time by the lake. It's a fitting conclusion: that there's merit in being different, inspiration in being individual, courage in being unique, and freedom in being yourself.

As Henry Thoreau said, "All good things are wild, and free".

DECEMBER

XIV

HOME FROM HOME

December is here and with it a return to normal life. I've packed away my tent, met Mrs H down by the dam, loaded the car and been chauffeured home. I've unpacked, washed, eaten, and settled into my favourite chair to read through eleven months' of journals. I have a glass of port in one hand and my favourite fountain pen in the other. Mrs H is sitting opposite and a log crackles and spits in the fireplace. I wish I could say that this is a perfect scene, but it's not. There's a grumbling and groaning coming from the washing machine in the kitchen that, despite its protestations, was force-fed a mouthful of stinking, nine-month-old clothes which it now seeks to wretch all over the floor.

The Journal rests upon my lap. It has the look of a book that has been buried for a century. Its boards are scuffed and splatted with mud; its pages are rippled with damp and soiled with the grime of outdoor existence. And it smells. It smells of wood smoke, a damp tent, mould spores and – something else. If I bring my nose closer to the pages I can detect a peaty whiff, not unlike an abandoned bird's nest. I don't know what it is but, I fear, once the journal is written up into neater handwriting, the original will be laid to rest – buried in

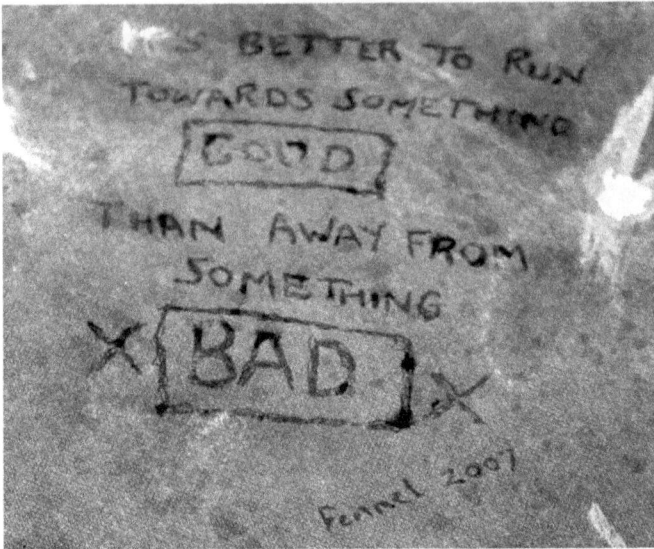

the garden to decompose slowly. Or, as is likely given its smell, to grow into an enormous mushroom.

Pretty soon I'll be enjoying my normal routine, going up into the attic to bring down the Christmas decorations. 'Old Satano' will still be there, fizzing and popping and flashing, trying to earn its place on top of the Christmas tree. The boxes in the loft will need to be brought down at some point, but alas, we've not yet found a buyer for our cottage. (For sale: Two-bedroom cottage. 'Requires modernisation.')

My objective this year was to rediscover the freedom and simple pleasures of childhood. By spending so much time by water, as I had done during my school years, I hoped that I could add to the contentment I'd found with Mrs H and amplify the 'Escape – Enjoy' messages of the Priory. I achieved this, finding freedom and relaxation, but I discovered how lonely it can be.

I learned how being isolated from a normal life, living for so long in the woods and orbiting a lake, made me yearn to be home, with my wife, and tending to my garden. The lake that was my home, that provided my food and the inspiration for this Journal, eventually reflected another world, far away. I realised just how selfish I'd been in my pursuit of escapism. Never again will I leave Mrs H alone for so long. It's not good for her, and it's not good for me. But I stand by my actions. Satnav will get us quickly and all-too-predictably from A to B, but the path of life is more interesting when we're allowed to explore the side streets, even if they lead back to our original location.

It's the special things close to home, and the breadth of life, that makes our time on this earth so valuable. My goal this year was to spend time by water, but I found that when an angler's blinkers are removed, a lake or river becomes part of a broader and more beautiful environment. Often I would turn away from the lake to study the woods and hedgerows, fields and streams. These held just as much interest and attraction. I would explore these places at dawn, and return to my camp at night without feeling like I had missed anything.

"It's better to run towards something good, than away from something bad." I wrote these words onto the cover of the journal after writing the 'Canehenge' piece. But in which direction was I running? My year in the woods feels, in retrospect, like I was putting other areas of my life on hold so that I could fulfil a whim. But it has allowed me to think clearly about what's important,

and the order in which things should and will be done. I doubt I'd have thought like this if I'd lived a normal year, commuting every day and getting progressively wearier from the tedium of work. Instead, I have become absolutely confident in the Priory. It has grown, matured, become more than it once was.

I knew last year that an adventure like this was not the best way to savour the Priory. But I did it anyway. Why? I could blame my work situation, but the honest answer is that I was trying too hard to fulfil the promise made in the last Journal. I didn't need to spend nine months living in the wild. A few weeks would have been plenty. A weekend might have sufficed. I sought happiness by the lake because I felt as though the job I was doing and the environment in which I worked had compromised my personal values and identity. I overcompensated. Quitting my job was a bold but rash thing to do. But disappearing into a wood during a year when I was moving house? That's nearly as bad as spending the first months of marriage living alone by a lake…

I stuck to my goal of getting close to nature. I certainly did that, but it wasn't without sacrifice or difficulty. I've experienced the desperate panic of being completely isolated (never, ever, eat wild mushrooms unless you absolutely know that they're safe to eat, and even then only when you have a way of making an emergency call should the worst happen); I've felt the toe-flinching terror of finding mice in my sleeping bag; endured the multi-swipe ineffectiveness of damp toilet paper; and the dread of knowing that my tent

only remains waterproof for the first twenty minutes of a downpour. All this for a sense of freedom? A man can never be truly free when he knows that he is neglecting his duties elsewhere.

An angling friend of mine, Peter Stone, once told me that the key to happiness is in keeping one's life in balance. This is so true. Whether we are a young sapling or ancient tree, we need a balanced diet of time by water and time away from water to keep us healthy. The trick is in knowing, and feeling, when the time is right to transition between the two.

Returning home, then, was the right thing to do. And, all things considered, is the highlight of my year.

No more selfishness. Just a balanced, contented, and richly meaningful life.

XV

THE COTTAGE POOL

Turning the first few pages of this year's Journal, I notice that I made a promise to you in January that remains unfulfilled. I said that I'd tell you the story of The Cottage Pool, the lake whose contour map inspired this year's adventure. So, after taking a sip of port, I ask in my best 'Watch with Mother' voice, "Are you sitting comfortably? Then I'll begin".

The Cottage Pool is a small and insignificant-looking farm pond. It doesn't contain any big fish and has never made any headlines. But to me it is the perfect pool. I may have fished prettier and more atmospheric lakes, but none competes with the sentiments I have for The Cottage Pool. You see, the pool has played an important role in my life from a young age.

My earliest memory is of The Cottage Pool. I can remember running down the farm track to the lake, tripping, falling, and fracturing my skull on a brick in the road. I was three years old. Strangely, I can't remember the pain or hospital ordeal that followed. All I remember is my excitement at seeing the lake and wanting to be there as quickly as my little legs could carry me. You see, even before I was an angler, The Cottage Pool proved irresistible. It called to me, knowing that I would be happiest when sitting beside its waters.

Usually I would drop everything to be there. I compromised my A-level exams by spending so much time by the pool. I turned down dates with adventurous girls because I wanted to listen to the woodpigeons cooing beside the lake. None of this was sacrifice. The pool was my world. My perfect, beautiful world.

As a child, even more so than today, I found it easier to be alone than in company. The Cottage Pool was my haven. I would cycle there from home and quickly lose myself in an adventure around its shores. It is where I learned to fish and understand the genuine magic of nature. Over time, the pool became my soul mate, my confidante, my best friend.

Then something happened. A betrayal so painful that I had to say farewell to The Cottage Pool. In fact, it's too painful for me to think about right now. First, I'll tell you about the lake, then build up to the moment of departure.

Built in the eighteenth century, The Cottage Pool was formed by damming a stream that flowed through a wooded valley in Shropshire. The result was a two-acre lake that provided fresh water to the livestock in the neighbouring fields and dirty water to the local manor house. The pool's dam provided access to a farmworker's cottage that overlooked the pool. Sadly, the cottage no longer exists (it was replaced by a larger farmhouse in the 1980s) but the pool still bears its name. While the farmhouse is now an imposing building, the pool and its surroundings have no aspirations of grandeur. They are what they are: a small farm pond fringed

with rhododendrons, willows, birch, oaks, larch, and alders; beds of aquatic bistort and reedmace grow in the water, sedges and soft rush line the lake's margins. It is a peaceful and sheltered spot. Calm in character and atmosphere, except at night when it can be sinister. I found that it was best visited during the day.

Passers-by would stop and gaze at the pool for longer than they intended, studying the reflections in the water, admiring the bird life in the trees and rejoicing at the displays of rhododendron flowers in spring. Then they would notice more subtle details – like damselflies flitting above the water, a heron standing in the margins, and buzzards mewing overhead. And, if they stared long enough, they'd detect the shadowy shapes of carp swimming by.

At the age of fourteen, I was invited to join the club that held the fishing rights to the pool. It was known to the committee that I worked part-time as a gardener and as such they saw my potential as a labourer at working parties. I was granted membership on the proviso that I worked as Fishery Manager at the pool. My responsibilities were to maintain access to the water, monitor catch returns, and increase wildlife diversity. I accepted the terms and set to work sensitively clearing fishing areas, building wooden jetties (things I now hate), coppicing willows, planting saplings (taken as cuttings from the trees surrounding famous carp lakes), sowing wildflower seeds, planting water lilies, relocating reeds, and dividing irises.

The most important management jobs were done in the spring, during the coarse fishing closed season.

This gave me an opportunity to be at the pool without any angling distractions. I kept watch on the nests of mallards, coots and moorhens (mindful of the ever-present threat of mink); I watched the fish spawn, saw the lapwings arrive and raise their young, and marvelled at the rhododendron blossom. It was a time of giving and receiving; ensuring the pool and its wildlife (including me) had the best start to the year.

My relationship with The Cottage Pool was as custodian, far more than angler. I loved being there, in all capacities, in all weather and at all times of the year. I only began thinking of fishing in June, when I would pre-bait my chosen swim for the start of the season. On the 16th June I would cycle to the lake at dawn, then sit and watch a float while I waited for a bite. My early catches consisted of skimmer bream, roach and gudgeon. Eventually I hooked a huge fish that, by complete fluke, avoided all the weed beds and overhanging branches and made it safely into my net. The fish – a 5lb wild carp – changed my world and set me on a course that would define the rest of my angling life. But that's another story.

Five years later, things at The Cottage Pool were changing. I was secretary of the club, with increasing responsibilities and a profound awareness of the politics of running an angling organisation. Most of the original members had become too old to fish and had relinquished their membership. Newer members didn't have the same sense of ownership as the founders and were less concerned with the long-term health of the pool. They just wanted to catch lots of fish and not be bothered with conservation or wildlife-centric expense. This coincided with a doubling of the rent, meaning that the club had to recruit new members from the 'second' waiting list (the one where people wait, usually with no chance of joining). Bringing in these people was to end my time at The Cottage Pool.

The new members had different ideals and interests. They outvoted the committee on subjects that had previously been taboo. Motions were passed to erect more platforms, coppice the rhododendrons, strip out the reeds and stock more fish (fortunately, wild carp from a Norman moat). The Cottage Pool faced a new era, one threatened by urgency, one-upmanship and disregard for nature.

Things came to a head during the following year when, at the Annual General Meeting, the members voted in favour of abolishing the closed season.

(The Government had recently permitted riparian owners to choose whether they allowed coarse fishing between March and June.) How could these people be so selfish and shortsighted? Why did they seek bland and seasonless fishing? How could anglers, the so-called guardians of nature, show such disregard for the overall wellbeing of the lake? My objections fell on deaf ears. The pool and its wildlife would no longer be protected by the three-month closed season. This most special time – when I would normally have the lake to myself – was no more. Anglers would be there. Fishing. Prowling the banks like a fox about to slaughter a house full of hens. Spring at the lake would no longer be a quiet time. The pool would not be allowed to wake slowly after a long winter. There would be no respite.

The black cap was placed; the gavel fell. I resigned my position on the committee, left the club, and walked away from The Cottage Pool, not knowing if I'd ever return. That was fourteen years ago: a long time separated from one's love. I've not fished there since, even though I've often thought about the pool, and wished her well. Would The Cottage Pool still be as beautiful as she once was? Would the lapwings still be there in spring and the woodpigeons be cooing in summer? Would the carp still patrol the edges of the lake at dawn and dusk? Would the lake still excite me, and make me want to run towards it? These are the questions I've asked every week since that fateful event. I know in my heart that they will, some day, need answering.

It is my destiny to return to The Cottage Pool.

THE LAST CAST

As an angler I'm entitled to one last cast, a final attempt to capture what I seek to convey. So here goes:

Being a gardener, I know that just enough water will bring a seed to life and sustain a plant into maturity. Too much water will rot the seed and leave a patch of stagnant earth. The same applies to the time one spends beside water. I hear that sailors crave dry land after too long at sea, and yet they desire the sea when on land. As an angler I've experienced both 'the parching' to be by water, and 'the drowning' when I know I've been by water for too long. When I was younger, it would take months for me to notice that I'd become submerged; now it can take minutes. The conclusion to which I've come is that one's time by water is cumulative, like an internal reservoir that is replenished. As we get older, our mental image of water becomes stronger, which fixes any leaks in the reservoir. We can go longer between visits, or visit for less time, because the image is already there. It doesn't need much topping up. This 'Lake Within' can be seen whenever we close our eyes and imagine a fresh sea breeze, or the trickling of a favourite stream, or the scent of a familiar pool.

I'll leave you with a story that proves my theory:

One of my closest childhood friends, a man named Bill Cross, was a keen salmon fisher. He would spin, float-fish a prawn, or cast a fly. It didn't matter. That he was by water was enough. Then he grew old and could no longer fish. The last time I saw Bill he was in his early nineties and sitting in his chair at home, with his Labrador at his feet. He'd not fished for years.

"I've brought you some magazines, Bill," I said. "*Trout & Salmon*, to help you overcome the parching."

Bill stared at me with cataract-clouded eyes, and then laughed.

"Oh, my boy, how kind; but I don't need these. I go fishing from my chair every day!"

Bill's reservoir was most definitely full, and crystal clear.

As I said at the start of this Journal, it is the power to dream that makes water so compelling.

ABOUT THE AUTHOR

FENNEL HUDSON

"Author, artist, naturalist and countryman. His is a lifestyle to inspire the most bricked-up townie."

Fennel Hudson is a lifestyle and countryside author known for his *Fennel's Journal* books and *Contented Countryman* podcasts. Born into a fishing family, he was never far from water. He was asked to manage his first fishery at the age of 15. He then looked after a further six lakes before starting a career in the corporate jungle. When things went badly wrong, he turned to the place where he felt safest: a 14-acre estate lake in Worcestershire. From having everything, to losing everything, he spent nine months beside the lake, rebuilding his life and his identity. This gave him a unique perspective of the true beauty (and humour) of life, which he shares by reminding us to 'Stop – Unplug – Escape – Enjoy'.

For more information please visit:
www.fennelspriory.com

THE FENNEL'S JOURNAL SERIES

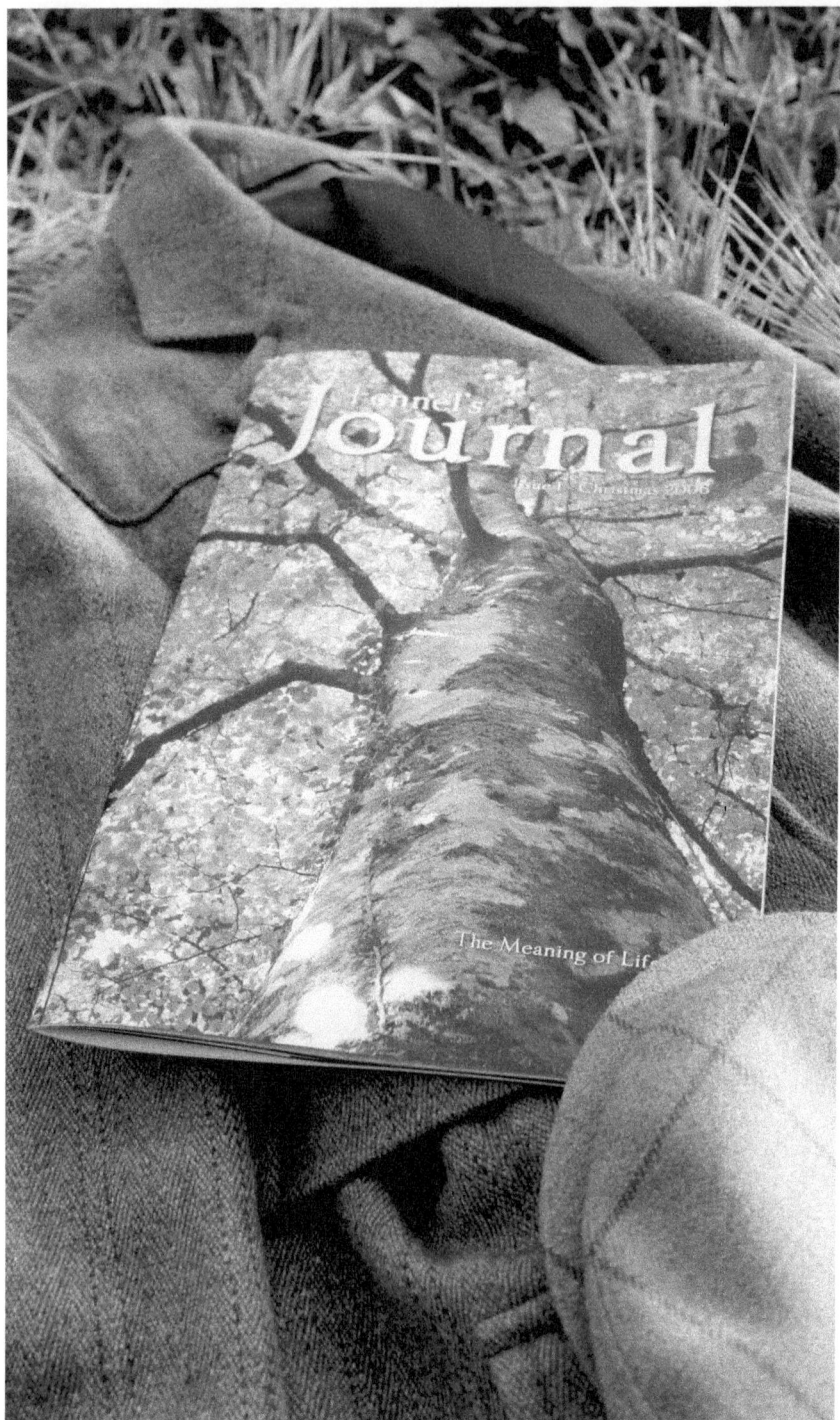

THE FIRST-EVER REVIEWS OF FENNEL'S JOURNAL:

"Fennel's Journal began as a series of illustrated letters to friends. As these evolved they became less a diary, more a manifesto, and the Journal is now exactly that – a way of living, rurally and simply: very real for all those who recognise the importance of tradition and joy."

Caught by the River

"I can see where it might lead. What he has would make amazing TV. It's the Good Life, but in a realistic way. It's Jack Hargreaves. It's Countryfile. It's quality Sunday newspaper stuff. It's 1948, all over again. In trying to escape the present he's inevitably created a brand. A potentially very powerful brand."

Bob Roberts Online

"Fennel's Journal is a masterpiece about rural living. It is a route-map to the life we all seek."

The Traditional Fisherman's Forum

From A Meaningful Life:

"Life is the most beautiful and rewarding gift. We just need to take time out to allow us to reflect, change perspective, and see things in their best light. Sometimes we just have to stop and feel the pulse of the Earth, the rhythm of the seasons and the internal voice that was once our childhood friend. As the natural world grows smaller, so too does its intensity and the size of the window through which it may be viewed."

NO.1

A MEANINGFUL LIFE

A Meaningful Life is the first and perhaps most important Journal. It documents the origins of Fennel's Priory and why Fennel decided to live by a new set of ideals. With themes ranging from escapism, adventure, work-life balance, identity and purpose, through to traditionalism and country living, it sets the scene for future editions – building messages that are central to Fennel's Priory. Ultimately it conveys the importance of a relaxed, balanced, and meaningful life.

READER TESTIMONIALS

"I loved reading this Journal. It's inspiring and has the beginnings of something very special."

"Fennel's chosen trajectory is firmly in the slow lane. He's a countryman, with courage to stand behind his traditional values."

"Witty and emotive, Fennel's writing conveys passion for a slower-paced and quieter life."

From A Waterside Year:

"Water is intrinsically linked to the
mystery and excitement of discovering
new worlds. Of dreams. And hopes.
And thoughts of what 'could be'.
Dreams free us from normality.
...As the daydreams grew longer, the
distinction between what was real and
what was imaginary grew less. Soon I
existed in a blissful world of my own
creation. Reality, as I learned, is only a
matter of perception...A life that is real
to one is surreal to another."

NO. 2

A WATERSIDE YEAR

In *A Waterside Year*, Fennel takes time out to live beside a lake in rural England. Here he appreciates the healing qualities of water, studies the wildlife around him, lives at the pace of someone outside of normal daily life, and discovers the freedom that's found in isolation. Getting so close to Nature, and spending time in idle fashion, enables him to discover a stronger sense of self. Ultimately he learns that freedom is not a place, but something that exists within us.

READER TESTIMONIALS

"A year in the wild. How we would all love to follow in Fennel's stead and indulge our dreams, to come out the other side a stronger and wiser person."

"A Journal with a message – that we should take time out to think about what's important, and see the beauty of the world."

"A truly blissful read full of inspiration and humour. The story of Fennel sitting in his tent, with the noises outside, had me laughing out loud!"

From A Writer's Year:

"Writing, with a fountain pen
and ink from a bottle, is the
simplest of things. Yet it can
transport us to a different
place entirely. Imagination is
the real magic that exists in
this world. Look inwards,
to see outwards. And
capture it in writing."

NO. 3

A WRITER'S YEAR

A Writer's Year celebrates the writer's craft. It champions the handwritten letter, discusses vintage pens and writing ink, and celebrates things such as antique typewriters and the quirkiness of the creative mind. It's a blend of observations. It's funny. It's serious. It's real life. But most of all it is written to encourage aspiring authors to find their voice, to put pen to paper, and follow their dreams.

READER TESTIMONIALS

"Worth it for the first chapter alone. It cannot fail to motivate and inspire the would-be author."

"What Fennel has written is not so much a eulogy for the handwritten letter as a call-to-arms for everyone to follow their dreams and make the most of their God-given talents. This is a genuinely inspiring read."

"I loved the part: 'If a pen can communicate our thoughts, dreams and emotions and be the voice of our soul, then ink is the medium that carries the message'. It shows how important and generous writing can be."

From Wild Carp:

"Some will say that searching for your
dreams is like looking for unicorns in
an emerald forest. They will say that
following a golden thread will lead
only to a king, dethroned and living
in the gutter. This may be so.
But the king was made, not born.
The crown was never his to wear.
...If ever the adventure proves tiring,
or you lose sight of your dream, look
to the west at sunset. There, on days
when the skies are clear, you might
see upon the horizon a thin layer of
golden mist. When it appears, you
will know its purpose: it is
the mist of believing."

NO. 4

WILD CARP

Angling for wild carp is about adventure, history, atmosphere and emotion. *Wild Carp* captures this aplenty, describing Fennel's 20-year quest to find a very special type of fish. But it's also about nature connection and a desire to uncover the seemingly impossible – a place where we can discover and live out our dreams, to completely indulge the mantra of 'Stop – Unplug – Escape – Enjoy'.

READER TESTIMONIALS

"When written well, traditional angling writing by the likes of BB, for example, is the type of literature that I can read again and again. Fennel's writing flows un-hurried without overly romanticising each point and the research is thorough; from the first sentence I was thinking, 'this lad can write!' It's informative and very refreshing."

"Such inspiring writing. His words 'Somewhere in the undergrowth of the impossible' had me staring out from the page in amazement. Fennel's writing is pure poetry."

From Fly Fishing:

"The deeper we travel into the natural world, and the greater the number of technological encumbrances we leave behind, the more likely we are to escape the fast-paced lifestyle and stresses of the 21st Century.
For some, angling enables a quest into the unknown, an adventure into the wild. For these fortunate folk, fly-fishing is escapism. Their hours by water serve as contemplation to enrich their souls, directing their quest inwards, towards their longed-for state of completeness."

NO. 5

FLY FISHING

Fly Fishing celebrates the most graceful and artful form of angling, explaining what it means to be an angler – in the spirit of Izaak Walton – and how fly fishers differ from bait fishers. The sporting and aesthetic beauty of fly-fishing is described in Fennel's usual witty and contemplative style. As he says, "Fly fishing is the ultimate form of angling; it gives us a reason to fish simply, travel lightly, and explore wild places that replenish our soul. With a fly rod, we're not casting to a fish; rather to a circle of dreams: ripples that spread into every aspect of our lives".

READER TESTIMONIALS

"Brilliant writing. Fennel made me laugh out loud in bed. My wife was asking questions!"

"A delightful, well-articulated, read. I strongly recommend it, especially to the contemplative, tradition-loving, bamboo fly rod devotees among us."

"A very inspiring and rewarding read. I will try to tie the Sedgetastic fly. It looks tasty!"

From Traditional Angling:

"Physics teaches us that for every action, there is an equal and opposite reaction: a natural balance of energy that sustains the equilibrium of life. In modern angling, these forces are skewed so far in favour of technology that the balance between science and art has been lost. But there is a movement, an undercurrent that defies the flow of progress. There are those who choose not to follow the crowd. They seek not to fish in a predictable, scientific manner. They yearn for the opposite, to buck the trend, *to be different.* They are the Traditional Anglers."

NO. 6

TRADITIONAL ANGLING

Traditional Angling celebrates the Waltonian values of angling: about fishing in a seasonal and uncompetitive way for the pure pleasure of being beside water. It wears its heart on its sleeve and a wildflower in its lapel. It's passionate, provocative and eccentric, written for those who appreciate the aesthetics of angling and uphold its sporting traditions. So, with great enthusiasm, raise your bamboo rod aloft for an adventure that proves there's more to fishing than catching fish.

READER TESTIMONIALS

"A beautifully written, very engaging and hugely enjoyable read. In fact, it's the best thing on fishing I've read in a long time."

"What a Journal! Fennel is clearly the spiritual successor to his mentor – the great Bernard Venables. There's so much wisdom and craftsmanship in his writing. Bernard clearly taught him very well."

From The Quiet Fields:

"The countryside, with its vast
horizons, fresh air and ever-changing
seasons is, by its very nature, more
life-giving and adventurous than any
amount of modern indoor living.
It inspires a love of natural history –
everything from the birds that sing in
the trees to the quality and richness
of the soil beneath our feet. Most
of all, it creates the desire to exist
more naturally. And in doing so, we
appreciate the balance of life."

NO. 7

THE QUIET FIELDS

The Quiet Fields is rooted in the humus-rich soil of the countryside. It's about remote rural places where Nature exists undisturbed, where we may sit and ponder 'The Wonder of the World'. The Journal tips its hat to these places, and to the nature writing of BB, revealing the 'Lost England' that still exists if you know where and how to look. It is the most sentimental and astutely observed Journal to date, discussing the 'true beauty' of Nature. If you've ever yearned to hear birdsong during a busy day, then this is the book for you.

READER TESTIMONIALS

"Fennel's writing reminds me of the works of Roger Deakin. It inspires me with faith in the quiet life and that although I may be isolated, I am certainly not alone."

"Fennel has captured the essence of the countryside – that is, its almost human character. So brilliantly has he compared and contrasted it with the nature of we humans. It's not so much a 'balanced study', more a 'study of the balance' between Nature and Man."

From Fine Things:

"It seems that, depending upon which side of the thesaurus-writer's gaze we sit, one's uniqueness as a person can be deemed to be either eccentric or distinctive. Both, in my opinion, are good...As we get older, and experience more things, those of us with strength of character and a sense of purpose will grow stronger and fight harder; those who lack identity and direction might end up sitting in a corner somewhere, blindly taking all the knocks that life throws at them. What does this teach us? That character and purpose are directly linked to confidence and conviction. What links them? Courage – to be oneself, no matter what others might say."

NO. 8

FINE THINGS

Fine Things celebrates the special and sentimental items and activities that convey our personality. The writing is fast-paced, quirky and humorous, reflecting the author's enthusiasm and eccentric view of the world. But be warned: if you look inside Fennel's mind, you might see a hula-hooping hamster named Gerald, shaking his maracas, loudly banging a bongo, and getting him into all sorts of trouble. So strap yourself in. This book picks up pace and takes some unexpected turns. From the deeply personal to the outright eccentric, it's for those who seek to be different.

READER TESTIMONIALS

"A very fine thing, indeed. Fennel's best and funniest book to date. He is the only author who can make me laugh out loud and cry in the same sentence. I was constantly in tears, for all the right reasons."

"Deep in places, outright bonkers in others. A demonstration of the fine line between genius and madness."

From A Gardener's Year:

"Roll up your sleeves and imagine
your vision of paradise. This, in
whatever form it takes, is your garden.
Keep hold of the image; know it's
every detail and piece together
the elements that need creating or
nurturing, so that when you get the
chance, you can prepare the ground,
sow the seeds, and make it real.
Ours is a gardener's life, whether we
realise it or not."

NO. 9

A GARDENER'S YEAR

A Gardener's Year celebrates the joy of growing things and reflects upon a life working with plants. But it's not a record of horticultural activities through the seasons. It's a metaphor for having a dream and making it come true. For Fennel, who has spent half his life working in gardens, it's about cultivating a cottage garden where he can aspire to a self-sufficient lifestyle. The Journal sees him sow the seeds of this future reality.

READER TESTIMONIALS

"Fennel's writing is uniquely funny. I mean, who else can name a chapter 'Chicken Poo'? His sense of humour, balanced with some deep yet subtle messages, had me in tears. From his 'escape' to a public toilet, to what not to say to a celebrity, this is a Journal to entertain all readers."

"When I started reading this Journal I had a garden with a lawn and a patio. Now I have a vegetable patch, blisters, an aching back, and the biggest smile of my life. Thank you Fennel!"

From The Lighter Side:

"If self-actualisation is the pinnacle
of one's development, then it can't be
achieved if your mountain has two
peaks...Being the 'best version' of
yourself implies that you have other
versions kept locked in a closet. Don't
have any 'versions'. Just have one true,
beautiful and pure form of you.
So climb your mountain, open your
arms to the Creator who greets you
there, and sing loudly to the world
that stretches out beneath you.
Write your name permanently on
the landscape of your mind.
Remember: you are a child of Nature.
And you are free."

THE LIGHTER SIDE

There's a delicate balance between something meaning a great deal and that same thing becoming so serious that it's ludicrous. (Ever got stressed about what clothes to wear for an interview?) That's why *The Lighter Side* provides the encouragement, humour, anecdotes, reflections and honesty that are essential to Fennel's message of 'Stop – Unplug – Escape – Enjoy'. After all, we can only 'Enjoy' if we know how to smile when we get there.

READER TESTIMONIALS

"The Lighter Side was more than I expected. The deeper meaning within it – and the devastating honesty it conveys – made me question exactly where I am in my own life and what I can do to improve it for my family and me in the time that remains. Thank you Fennel for opening my eyes and adjusting my course."

"The opening chapter is the most startling, erudite, compassionate and open piece of writing I have ever read…thank you Fennel for sharing so much. It did and does mean a great deal."

From Friendship:

"What I'm talking about is proper friendship. The sort that is authentic, genuine and real. Where we can look into the eyes of another person and know what they're thinking. ...Because, as friends, we remember 'why' as much as 'when' or 'what'. Through good times and bad, we were there. Together. That's the bond, the unquestionable obligation that's freely given. It's the tightest hug, the biggest kiss, the tearful hello and the widest smile. If that's what it means to be a friend, or an extrovert, or just someone who cares for others then that's me to the last beat of my heart."

NO. 11

FRIENDSHIP

Written by the Friends of the Priory, with bonus chapters from Fennel, *Friendship* provides insights into what it means to be friends, how shared interests and beliefs support collective purpose, and how, when we're together, we can achieve more, appreciate more, and have more fun. It's about the broader world of Fennel's Priory and how it exists in others. It's a book written 'for us by us', with friendship as the theme.

READER TESTIMONIALS

"Possibly the greatest gift that this Journal bestows is to let us know that we are not alone."

"Like friendship itself, this Journal brings together people and meaning. It reminds us that 'together we are strong'. Thank you Fennel for leading our charge."

"The message (and evolution) of Fennel's Journal is most evident in this Friendship edition. With such obvious themes as identity and legacy, it's clear that what Fennel has shared over the years is a route-map to freedom and a stronger sense of self."

From Nature Escape:

"I am once again seeking an escape,
to where I hope to find freedom and
connect with the young man who
handed me his trust ten years ago.
This will be a faithful interpretation
of the Priory, a fitting way to mark ten
years of writing. As I said at the end
of last year's Journal, 'One's journey
through life is not linear; it's circular.'
So let's go back to the beginning,
and rediscover the quiet world."

NO. 12

NATURE ESCAPE

Nature Escape provides the most detailed account of a day that follows the motto of 'Stop – Unplug – Escape – Enjoy'. In it Fennel returns to the woodland of his youth to study its wildlife and savour its peacefulness.

Written in real-time, with twenty-four chapters that each represent an hour, the Journal is an account of how time spent outdoors in wild places enables us to observe the nature that's around us *and* within us.

READER TESTIMONIALS

"Fennel's Journal has always provided us with an escape, but now we know where the escape can lead. As promised, it leads to enjoyment – and very enjoyable it is too!"

"24 hours alone in a wood, with only 'the wild' for company? With Fennel as our guide, there's no such thing as 'alone'; only the warmth of knowing that quiet times are the fine times."

"By studying the nature within us and around us, Fennel demonstrates how to be 'at one' with nature."

From Book of Secrets:

"There's a greater man than me
who can sum up our journey, a
mountaineer who in 1865 first
climbed the Matterhorn. Edward
Whymper, over to you: 'There have
been joys too great to be described
in words, and there have been griefs
upon which I have not dared to dwell,
and with these in mind I say, climb if
you will, but remember that courage
and strength are naught without
prudence, and that a momentary
negligence may destroy the happiness
of a lifetime. Do nothing in haste,
look well to each step, and from
the beginning think what may
be the end.'"

NO. 13

BOOK OF SECRETS

Book of Secrets links all editions of Fennel's Journal together. With 14 Journals in the series, and 14 core chapters in this book, it's the 'one book to bind them all' with each chapter providing the continuity story from one Journal to the next.

Containing Fennel's previously private writing, it provides deep insight into the Fennel's Journal story. If you've ever wondered why each Journal is themed the way it is, or tried to find the metaphor in each edition, then *Book of Secrets* is for you.

READER TESTIMONIALS

"What a privilege: being able to read the private writing of my favourite author. Book of Secrets is a treat."

"Such honesty and wit. Fennel puts into words what I have only ever thought, or dare not say."

"Fennel's Journal really is a series – it's meant to be read as a whole. And now we have the key to unlock it."

From The Pursuit of Life:

"We can hide, or we can strive – for a life of our making. With endless possibilities and opportunities to reach for our dreams, we owe it to ourselves to dream big and keep going, irrespective of what we might encounter. Sadly, the thing that most limits our success is not others, but ourselves. How strongly we believe, how confidently we act, how fiercely we react, how passionately we want, and how life-affirmingly compelled we are to grow and blossom; that's how we keep going, no matter what, to be the person we want to be, living the life we deserve, in dreams that are real."

NO. 14

THE PURSUIT OF LIFE

The Pursuit of Life concludes the Fennel's Journal story. It's a reflective tome that provides Fennel's commentary on the journey and a 'behind the scenes' view of the challenges and rewards of a life rebuilt on one's terms.

It's an account of how the series came to be and how it evolved, and includes much of Fennel's private writing, several of the original handwritten drafts, correspondence between The Friends, and encouragement for those on similar paths. Ultimately it shows how the Fennel's Journal series can be used as a route map to a more fulfilling life.

READER TESTIMONIALS

"A life retold, for our benefit. Fennel is to be congratulated for everything he's achieved – on paper and in life."

"It's his life in the books, but it could so very easily be ours. Fennel has a way of seeing truth in the severe and the sublime, and bringing it home."

"Can this really be the end? When dreams are real, we never wake from them. More books Fennel, please!"

www.ingramcontent.com/pod-product-compliance
Lightning Source LLC
Chambersburg PA
CBHW031534260326
41914CB00032B/1796/J